Praise for *The 24-Hour Rule*

"It's hard to perform well and feel like you belong in an organization when you have no idea what's going on or how to get your work done. *The 24-Hour Rule* is a wonderful guidebook for creating dynamic documentation that works from the day-to-day work you and your team are already doing. Read it, make dynamic documentation a team habit, and watch your team's performance and belonging soar."

—Charlie Gilkey, bestselling author of *Start Finishing*

"If you think implementing and improving documentation in your business is something you can put off to 'when you have time,' you are putting your business at risk, stalling growth, and missing one of the most powerful instruments of scale. *The 24-Hour Rule* gives you a crystal-clear path to unlocking value, creating team alignment, and building the foundation for your business to grow with ease."

**—Pamela Slim, award-winning author of
Body of Work and *The Widest Net***

"*The 24-Hour Rule* provides an exceptional framework and intensely well-thought-out steps, examples, arguments, and processes to cure our docu-phobia (or, just as bad, our docu-zealotry) and to capture and share what we know, learn, and invent. The approach is easy to read yet dense enough that I found myself taking notes and stopping to consider its applications and what I could do better."

—Jason Cassidy, CEO, Shinydocs and AIIM Board Member

"Insightful and applicable, *The 24-Hour Rule* is a guide for workers and business leaders alike in a world where the volume of information and data in an organization is growing exponentially."

—Tim Brady, CEO, Colligo

"Simple, powerful, and compelling . . . Bellehumeur shows the vital nature of documentation in building our personal credibility and how the 24-Hour Rule will make you stand apart among your peers. No fluff, just example after example of knowledge tools you can put to use right away, presented in a way you'll find hard not to binge read."

—Brian Bench, former CIO, CNOOC International

The 24-HOUR RULE

The
24-HOUR
RULE

and Other Secrets
for Smarter Organizations

Adrienne Bellehumeur

Matt Holt Books
An Imprint of BenBella Books, Inc.
Dallas, TX

Matt Holt is an imprint of BenBella Books, Inc.
10440 N. Central Expressway
Suite 800
Dallas, TX 75231
benbellabooks.com
Send feedback to feedback@benbellabooks.com

BenBella and *Matt Holt* are federally registered trademarks.

Printed in the United States of America
10 9 8 7 6 5 4 3 2 1

Library of Congress Control Number: 2022038264
ISBN 9781637742839 (hardcover)
ISBN 9781637742846 (electronic)

Editing by Katie Dickman
Copyediting by Leah Baxter
Proofreading by Jenny Rosen and Madeline Grigg
Indexing by Amy Murphy
Text design and composition by PerfecType, Nashville, TN
Interior illustrations by Faceout Studio, Paul Nielse
Cover design by Brigid Pearson
Printed by Lake Book Manufacturing

To my husband, Neil,
and my kiddos Claire, Bruce, and Gwen,
who remind me of the importance of every 24 hours that we have.

CONTENTS

INTRODUCTION

Welcome to *The 24-Hour Rule and Other Secrets for Smarter Organizations*. I have spent the past fifteen years helping individuals, teams, and organizations work smarter, faster, and better—to solve problems, implement systems, set up rock-solid processes, unstick paralyzed projects, fight needless wheel spinning, and leverage all the information they already have (in their minds, offices, and digital files) to turn information garbage into gold.

You'll soon learn the same powerful techniques I use with my clients. I'll show you how to use the practice of documentation to move your business forward and to create documents and systems that are actually useful and *(gasp!)* fun to read.

No matter what your situation—your files are a mess; you can't get your team to follow up; you're stuck in a vortex of meetings; no one reads your processes; your fancy system was a bust; your expensive, "best-in-class" consultants failed to deliver real change—I wrote this book so you can work *smarter.* I call the practice I teach "Dynamic Documentation," because it's all about taking control of your work to achieve your goals.

Think of it as equal parts art, science, discipline, and practice. Dynamic Documentation synthesizes key tenets of Information Management, Organizational Design, and Personal Productivity, always with a bias toward *action*. Documentation has traditionally been viewed as "static." That is, lifeless piles of paper, dusty binders on a shelf, records in your database. But when applied properly, documentation is "dynamic." It actively moves you forward and changes outcomes.

All of us "do" documentation—emailing, proposals, memos, spreadsheets, organizing our receipts, storing our files. But do we really "get" documentation? Experience tells us no. We often have little understanding of how we can apply the everyday skills of documentation—which we already know—to turbocharge our effectiveness. No matter what your business, industry, profession, or role is, whether you're a large company, a small company, or a solopreneur, you'll benefit from the tools taught in this book. You'll learn why the practice of documentation really is a superpower.

A bit about me: I am a consultant and business owner. My firm, Risk Oversight, is based in Calgary, Alberta, and specializes in Internal Control and Compliance programs in the accounting space. I developed my documentation approach from tackling business analyst assignments, SOX (Sarbanes-Oxley) programs, Information Management projects, technical and proposal writing, communications, change management advising, and more. The methods I teach represent years of work with myriad professionals, including accountants, lawyers, engineers, administrators, sales professionals, project managers, IT people, large companies, small business owners, and more. My documentation approach is tried and proven across hundreds of client projects and (of course) many documents.

I will readily admit that, early in my career, the whole concept of "documentation" did *not* come easily to me. I drowned under stacks of papers, methodologies, and jargon. I'd go to meetings but didn't know what the heck to do after them. As a newly minted CPA, I documented for audits and accounting assignments, but I didn't see the point of what I was doing. I was lost and bounced around between jobs in my twenties.

It wasn't until I figured out that I wasn't the only one confused and overwhelmed by documentation that I saw how I could make it better. As I practiced new habits and applied them to my work, the "secrets" of *The 24-Hour Rule* were born. The 24-Hour Rule (which you'll learn in chapter three is about doing *something* with information within 24 hours of hearing it) is a core concept of my 6-step approach to "dynamic" documentation because you need to get things out of your head and onto paper (or your digital notes) to drive momentum and capture intellectual capital before—poof!—your short-term memory lets it go.

Over the years, I have come to understand that it's not your technical skills or the latest buzzword that makes you effective in what you do. It is committing to an unsung, everyday practice that makes you truly successful. Dynamic Documentation is a big part of that underlying practice.

I have used Dynamic Documentation to go from stumbling and bored in meetings to an oracle of information—and to go from crushed by templates, lingo, and technologies to forging my own structures for major clients. *The 24-Hour Rule and Other Secrets for Smarter Organizations* gives you these abilities too.

In part one, you'll learn the fundamental principles of Dynamic Documentation. In part two, you'll learn the 6 Steps of Dynamic Documentation, the "secrets" that will change your approach to work, and how to apply them to your team and your organization. In part three, you'll see how it looks when you put Dynamic Documentation into practice.

Ready to unleash your team's abilities and turn conversation into action? Ready to make your documentation practices an integral part of moving your team forward? Ready to tackle big problems and take on big opportunities in your organization? Then get passionate about documentation and encode Dynamic Documentation within your organization's DNA. It is my sincere hope that you will use Dynamic Documentation to improve your team and your organization and, in the process, improve your career and fulfill your personal goals, too.

PART
1

—

The Foundation

CHAPTER 1

What Is Dynamic Documentation and Why Does It Matter?

Smarter organizations don't just "do" documentation, they "get" it.

I f we want to work smarter, faster, and better—both solo and as teams—it is my firm belief and my experience with hundreds of client projects that we need a way to capture and act on everything on our plates at work and at home. To do this, we must listen to people, take good notes, and turn those conversations into action. We must follow these steps along with simple "rules" consistently.

Dynamic Documentation is a practice that shows us how to transform those unthinking, often mundane tasks into a system that drives momentum. It considers documentation a foundational tool for effective productivity and workflow that boosts the impact of our efforts.

Whether we realize it or not, documentation underpins a lot of what we do every day at work, including meetings, following up, organizing, writing emails, planning projects, writing processes and procedures, and generally pushing forward whatever we are working on.

When you hear the word "documentation," your mind probably goes to one aspect of work or another depending on your background and role.

Roles of Documentation

☑ **If you work in a large company...**
documentation might mean standards, systems, policies, and working across departments.

☑ **If you run a small business...**
documentation might mean your marketing, accounting, and customer information.

☑ **If you work in a start-up...**
documentation might mean building processes and practices from scratch to accelerate speed to market.

☑ **If you are in IT...**
documentation might mean systems documentation, network diagrams, configuration, code, incident and change management records, and business continuity.

☑ **If you work in the project or program management space...**
documentation might mean project plans, project templates, requirements gathering, and project communications.

☑ **If you are in finance or accounting...**
documentation might mean financial processes, journal entries, records of accounts payable and accounts receivable, investor presentations, and Internal Controls over Financial Reporting (ICFR).

☑ **If you are lawyer...**
documentation might mean contracts, legal opinions, policies, resolutions, and board minutes.

☑ **If you are in sales...**
documentation might mean follow-up with clients, lead generation, request-for-proposal materials, and marketing collateral.

At its simplest level, the "static but necessary" form of documentation is a "document" which can be any written, printed, or electronic piece that serves as evidence or as a record. This means anything from an accounting memo to the notes in your notebook to your birth certificate to the safety procedures in a warehouse. A document is a tangible product. Dynamic Documentation is a conduit to bigger, better, and bolder things.

REFRAMING DOCUMENTATION: THE CORE CONCEPTS OF DYNAMIC DOCUMENTATION

Dynamic Documentation is based on *lean* concepts, which means creating more value (i.e., money, quality, sales, momentum, peace of mind) from less effort (i.e., staff, time, systems, complexity, consultants). This means the documentation process is iterative, agile, and "good enough." Dynamic Documentation is not about making your files pristine, employing state-of-the-art technology, or documenting every task or detail. Nor is it about going down rabbit holes of your metadata or templates.

Dynamic Documentation is a *purpose-driven* practice. We document to drive action. If you write "call Mom" on your to-do list, are you more likely to do it? Probably. At every step, for every new system, process, or task we document, we need to ask: Will this move things forward? Will it help me or those who will be using it? Will it influence people's behaviors the way I want it to, now and in the future? Will it help others do their jobs better?

Documentation as a driver of action is a radical change from the traditional view of documentation as a drag on efficiency and progress. Some see documentation as a burden or as something that slows a project. This couldn't be further from the truth. Have you ever worked on a team where no one writes anything down? (I have pulled my hair out with these teams many times.) No one knows or remembers what was said in the previous meeting, so we have another meeting. And the cycle of futility rages on. (Or, in the context of a team of information specialists, the Information Management life cycle spins out of control.)

BIG D AND LITTLE D

There's one more important nuance to understanding the elements of Dynamic Documentation—the myth that documentation is always capital-D documentation that takes teams of IT, systems, and Information Management experts to design and implement.

Documentation can be created and managed by anyone by recording basic information in any place, like your notebook. You don't need to be an expert in Big Data, SharePoint, journalism, or records management to use and leverage the skills of documentation

Which brings me to "Little d." If "Big D" is about how we traditionally see documentation—records, formal systems, Information Management programs, policies, procedures, rules, and requirements, Little d is about the everyday practices and skills you and your team use, like your notes, to-do lists, emails, informal communications, and the skills to make this all happen.

If you are in the corporate world or go to conferences, you probably hear a lot about Big D initiatives—innovation programs, information governance, change management, corporate minutes, and so on. But it's those Little d skills and actions that keep Big D projects running.

You might have heard that "culture eats strategy for breakfast." Well, I say that "Little d eats Big D for lunch."

Don't forget Little d. Seriously. If you are at a conference and you fail to record the name of a new contact (a Little d practice), this person will never get in your sales funnel, you will never send them a proposal, you will never sign a contract with them, you will never send them an invoice, and you will never generate client files from them (all Big D results).

We need to understand the full spectrum of formality, from rigid corporate systems (Big D) to the sticky notes on your computer (Little d), to no "D" at all (i.e., ideas in your head).

Little d is about moving up the continuum from no D at all to getting your ideas, actions, thoughts, history, prospects, and opinions on paper to making

Big D / Little d

	●●●▶ LITTLE d EATS BIG D FOR LUNCH
Records	Emails
Corporate systems	Apps on your phone
Information governance	Personal workflow management
Formal processes	Meeting notes
Project management	To-do lists
Policies	Organizing your team's files
Corporate file structure	Everyday information sharing
Documentation requirements	Documentation skills

yourself heard and seen while relieving the mental burden of carrying too much in your head. At the other end of the spectrum, Big D projects come with all their big terms, high-end tools, and consultants. But before being dazzled by Big D's promises, you need to size up Little d's bench strength. This book will teach you a wide range of Little d skills and concepts to apply to (and be wildly successful at) your Big D projects and company goals.

A core aspect of understanding Dynamic Documentation as a practice is recognizing that all documentation, from formal to informal and big to little, plays an important role in getting everyone to work faster, smarter, and more nimbly.

INTRODUCING THE 24-HOUR RULE

You've just learned that Little d is the foundation of success for your projects and your career. So, let's now introduce the mother lode of Little d skill and discipline (and also the golden rule of documentation): the 24-Hour Rule.

Picture this situation (trust me, we've all been here): You hold an important meeting with your boss, leadership team, or a key client on a Friday afternoon before a long weekend. You've been trying forever to secure this meeting and it was the only time that worked. It was a successful meeting with many great ideas, action items, new concepts, opportunities, and points for further discussion.

But *after* the meeting, it's the *long* weekend! (Drinks!) You jump in the car with your friends (or family or whatever situation you're in) for three days of wine, sun, and fun.

Returning to work Tuesday morning, sitting happily in the office for some camaraderie and collaboration or WFH (working from home), depending on your current arrangement, you tell coworkers about your weekend, post pics on Instagram, check the news, roll into a check-in meeting, and grab your second Starbucks.

Before you know it, it's the afternoon.

Uh-oh. It's time to get on those notes. So, you stare at them, now a solid 96 hours after your meeting. Between your sleep-deprived glances (and mild lingering hangover), you can't quite remember the context or nuances of the chicken scratch or half-typed words in front of you. There goes your chance to impress your boss or client.

For most people, the situation is worse—they don't bother to *ever* write down an important meeting with their management or key client, which sooner or later ends up haunting them.

Does this situation sound familiar? If it does, you're not alone. I have laid out this scenario in presentations many times, including to senior people and successful entrepreneurs who have found themselves in this situation more times than they'd like to admit.

Early in my career, this situation plagued my work weekly, if not daily. I learned the hard way from not writing things down. I have been embarrassed, lost credibility, wasted some time (OK, a *lot* of time), and had to repeat meetings (with my proverbial tail between my legs).

I crafted this rule to save my career.

The 24-Hour Rule

states that you *must* rethink, reprocess, or rewrite
information within 24 hours of hearing it. (Or in simpler
terms: Just do *something* with the information.)

For the record, there are "other" 24-Hour Rules out there. There is one for airline tickets (where you have 24 hours to cancel a flight booked without penalty) and one for anti-money laundering legislation in Canada (where multiple transactions need to be aggregated when they are greater than $10K within a 24-hour window). And more commonly, there is the mindfulness practice of waiting 24 hours before acting when you are emotionally heated, about to reprimand someone, or making a big decision.

But *this* 24-Hour Rule is your ultimate Little d personal Information Management discipline. It is an essential part of moving your Big D projects forward, too, by grabbing information at the source and eradicating confusion, apathy, and rework. And it's your newest productivity hack.

The 24-Hour Rule takes us deeply into the psychology of Dynamic Documentation.

THE DISCIPLINES OF DYNAMIC DOCUMENTATION

The practice of Dynamic Documentation goes beyond the 24-Hour Rule. To fix your problems at hand, you also need to understand where you might be falling short within the holy trinity of documentation—information, process, and people. Or, what I call the Documentation Triad.

Dynamic Documentation is at the center of three core disciplines: Information Management (information), Organizational Design (process), and Personal Productivity (people), as shown in the following graphic. And each of these fields play a critical part in Dynamic Documentation. Let's explore.

The Documentation Triad

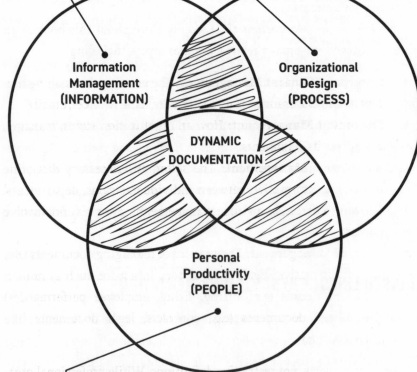

Big data, transformation
Contracts
Patents
Data, systems, metadata
Content management
Document management
Accounting records,
  purchase orders, invoices
Engineering records
Records management
Administrative records
Legal documents

Business processes,
  procedures, policies
Business analysis
Management reporting
Audits
Sales, requests for proposal
SOX and ISO
Systems documentation,
  data models, architecture
Project documentation
Corporate communications

**Information
Management
(INFORMATION)**

**Organizational
Design
(PROCESS)**

**DYNAMIC
DOCUMENTATION**

**Personal
Productivity
(PEOPLE)**

Personal knowledge management
Storing notes and ideas
Writing
Meeting notes
Interviewing
Document training
To-do lists

Writing for work
Personal brainstorming,
  mind mapping
Goal setting, resolutions
Sharing notes
Health, well-being, journaling
Personal finances, home management

Information (Information Management)

Taking Control of Existing Information

If your team takes forever to find things or you have clunky systems and scattered documents, your problem is in the Information Management circle of the Documentation Triad.

Information Management is the art of taking information (usually data or documents) and transforming it into something of value. Information Management is about organizing your documents and information and making them easy to use. In its simplest from, this could mean cleaning up your file folders. At a complex level, this could mean integrating disparate enterprise-wide systems.

I use *Information Management* (IM) loosely throughout this book as an umbrella term covering many related, popular topics, including:

- **Enterprise Content Management:** The practice of managing content in its various forms (e.g., documents, data, invoices, email)
- **Document Management:** How an organization stores, manages, and tracks its documents
- **Knowledge Management:** The softer, still-necessary discipline of sharing information between individuals, teams, departments, and divisions (i.e., knowledge management may or may not involve documentation)
- **Records Management:** The practice of managing documents that are administrative, legal, or regulatory in nature, such as human resources records (e.g., hiring, firing, employee performances) and official documents (e.g., contracts, legal documents like incorporation)

These are concepts, not restrictive definitions. While professional organizations such as ISO (International Organization for Standardization) or AIIM (Association for Intelligent Information Management) take a technical approach, in practice, these concepts grow a life of their own in organizations, professions, or teams.

The CEO doesn't care whether you call a project "Enterprise Content Management" or "Document Management." The concerns of a CEO are practical and immediate; that is, finding things when needed, legal protection for the company and themselves, and maximizing their ROI (return on investment).

Information Management is a broad professional discipline full of terms, lingo, and technologies to learn. It is a growing professional field, and the lingo is changing every year.

Documentation and Information Management are cousins. One is not a subset of the other. You need great documents to start Information Management. As we say, "garbage in, garbage out," or GIGO. The stronger your documents, the stronger your Information Management. Information Management, in turn, gives us the rules, technology, and processes, so your team can share and find what they need. Additionally, the stronger the listening, research, reporting, and problem-solving skills of an Information Management team, the more responsive and effective their projects become.

In today's large organizations, Information Management is reserved for professionals or teams dedicated to running this type of work. (It is entirely Big D.) Most of us don't "do" Information Management as part of our work. But most of us "do" documentation in some form or another. Documentation is a practice for everyone. You can dress documentation up and you can dress it down. You don't need fancy systems or methodologies to get started. You just need a pen and paper.

Information Management Practices include:
- Records management and administration (e.g., health-care records, human resources)
- Accounting records, purchase orders, invoices
- Legal documents, regulations, compliance, audit support
- Engineering drawings, design, code, specifications
- Data, systems, workflow, metadata
- Managing your team's files
- Managing the knowledge within your team and your organization

Process (Organizational Design)

Structure to Keep Your Organization Running Smoothly

If your sales team has no way to follow up on leads, your IT folks struggle with why systems go down, or your orders are mishandled, your problem is in the Organizational Design circle.

Organizational Design is another umbrella term for how organizations structure their tasks, people, systems, and processes. Organizational Design is the infrastructure that allows your organization to achieve its goals. It is about making your team, project, or company more efficient and effective, or smarter.

In your organization and industry circles, you are probably using one term or a combination of trendier (Big D) terms. Maybe it's "Business Process Reengineering," "Process Efficiency," "Value-Chain," "Streamlining," or "Transformation." Your consultants, eager to "unpack" their bleeding-edge expertise, will no doubt have you believe they know what's hip. (Last year, it was "Optimization," and then "Transformation" came into vogue.)

No matter what name you call it, what your consultants relabel it as this year, or how they jazz it up, Organizational Design projects boil down to the same concepts. They are all founded on the basic principles of:

- Documenting what *should* be done
- Documenting what *is* being done
- Identifying the gaps
- Addressing the gaps
- Monitoring and enforcing what you have changed

Documentation is the foundation of all Organizational Design projects. You need documentation to "design" how your processes should work, what your teams need to do, and how they should do it. Organizational Design projects that skimp on documentation are futile. You are left with big promises and no results.

In 2019, the Everest Group reported a failure rate of 73 percent on digital transformation projects. This wasn't because of a lack of big consulting names, fancy PowerPoints, or cool talking points, either. This was a failure of the basics (aka, Little d). Without Little d's practical guidance, Big D gets taken to places it doesn't want to go.

Little d practices like note-taking, interviewing, document creation, follow-up, emailing, and strong meetings make these word-of-the-year projects successful. (In fact, if Little d is good, you'll find the need for a lot fewer Big D projects.)

While Information Management is focused on records and administrative documentation, Organizational Design documentation is focused on items that bring clarity, momentum, and value, such as systems, processes, and practices. This is the documentation that is (or should be) ingrained in the fabric of your daily work life.

Organizational Design Practices include:
- Business processes, procedures, policies, training manuals
- Meeting notes, meeting agendas, meeting presentations
- Project plans, charters, requirement gathering
- Systems documentation, data models, network and architecture models
- Management reporting, financial and operational reporting
- Sales, request-for-proposal materials, prospecting, and lead tracking
- SOX, ISO, and other compliance programs
- Corporate communications, project communications, team communications

People (Personal Productivity)

How You and Your Team Get Work Done

If you're stuck in soul-sucking meetings, your team is stacked with talent but can't get anything done, or you have burned through ten different business analysts (or information managers, auditors, administrators, consultants, and so on) in the last two years, your problem is in the Personal Productivity circle of the diagram.

Personal Productivity is all about Little d—your and your team's writing skills, where you keep things, how you process information, and how you approach to-do items.

Most work problems have less to do with your information or processes and stem more from your people. In my experience, companies put too much emphasis on fancy systems, processes, and policies and not nearly enough priority on changing habits and behaviors.

You need to hire, fire, and train for documentation skills. You need to build your team's documentation mindset, too. Here's what I mean:

- If your sales people fail to record ideas from customer meetings, or fumble lead-generation opportunities, it delivers a direct hit to your bottom line.
- If your investor relations team is reinventing the wheel for every presentation, it's misallocating their time and energy.
- If you can't get your people to document their processes or leave a trail of what they are working on, it will hurt your ability to train others and scale your business.

Personal Productivity is about making you and your people more productive to achieve your goals. This is like Organizational Design, except applied to you and your team members individually, not collectively.

Experience teaches us that "what gets documented gets improved." Documentation changes human behavior. This is not pop psychology or fluffy stuff. This is a real-life, baked-into-the-cake truism based upon my years of industry experience.

Imagine if you asked your team members to record what they ate that week and then told them you will post their results on the whiteboard in your conference room, in the company newsletter, or on the corporate intranet at the end of the week. What do you think would happen? First, most people would lie (at least a bit). Some would feel embarrassed. Some would love the assignment. And guess what? Everyone would eat better that week. Even if they lied. This is just how human behavior works. An expectation to record and report leads to tangible results. Documentation changes how we act.

Documentation makes you more productive at work and in your personal life. It's a discipline that develops like a muscle. The more you work it, the stronger it grows. Fail to work at it and the muscle atrophies. Documenting puts you in a mental space for productivity and success. No matter your education, credentials, ambitions, or background, documentation forces a mindset that *makes things happen.*

If you attend a conference, listen to a webinar, or exhibit at a trade show, and your team fails to record a brilliant idea for your business, is this a reflection on the organizer or on your documentation discipline? Let's be honest, we might blame the conference, but it's usually on us.

Documentation takes skill and stamina, including a consistent focus that not everyone can stick to. But for those willing to put in the effort, the rewards are exponential for *any* career. Strong documentation skills ensure that:

- You are trusted.
- You drive momentum on your projects.
- Your competence is noted.
- You are confident in every situation.
- You are organized and prepared.
- You are more helpful to coworkers and clients.
- You are a better communicator.
- You solve problems faster.
- You complete tasks and projects.
- You are perceived as possessing an amazing superpower.

Focusing on the Personal Productivity aspect of documentation helps us to be realistic, not academic or theoretical, in our approach to documentation. We are practical in our personal lives. We buy what we need. We handle necessary, "unsexy" tasks for our families, houses, and finances. We buy technologies we want to use. Yet too often we throw this out the window when we get to work.

If your company's onboarding package is so detailed and boring that no one reads it, it may be technically correct, but it has failed to help the people who need it. If your team hosts an all-day workshop when a 30-minute interview would yield the same conclusions, then they aren't being smart. If your department implements a "state-of-the-art" incident management system that is more cumbersome to manage than your previous (albeit less sexy) system, they too don't "get it" when it comes to Personal Productivity and how it feeds into the big picture.

Without that connection to Personal Productivity—day-to-day reality and behavior—documentation can't help your company like it should. That is why it is folly to separate the concepts of Personal Productivity from documentation practices.

Personal Productivity Practices include:
- To-do lists, time management, goal setting
- Education, training, capturing ideas
- Interviews and meetings
- Recording and sharing notes, team-wide communications
- Health and well-being
- Managing personal work files
- Personal finances, managing home and family
- Motivational writing and journaling

THE BIGGER "WHYS" OF DYNAMIC DOCUMENTATION

Most of us can agree that documentation is a good business practice. But few see documentation as a superpower to improve their work, their team, and their organizations. Let's take a deeper look at why documentation matters and why we need to "get" documentation (and not just "do" it).

Add Value to Your Organization—Getting Maximum Results from Your Efforts

Documentation, when done properly, takes your ideas, processes, and practices, and turns them into tangible tools for growth. Documentation—like sales contacts, project materials, templates, training for staff—gives the power to replicate and build your business in new markets, with new customers, through new staff, and with new products and services. These are all reasons (among others) why documentation becomes an asset that positions your organization for success, now and into the future.

You don't need to be a major company to achieve results here. Blogs, articles, marketing materials, and so on are assets that add value to all companies, whether you are a Fortune 500 company or a solopreneur.

Dynamic Documentation is an investment that pays off. It creates a measurable business asset.

To my accountants in the house, pop quiz: What is the first element of the definition of an "asset"? (Answer: It has future value.) Documentation is something that truly does have a *future value*.

There are obvious examples of how documentation increases the future value of your organization.

One example is obtaining a patent, a process in which documentation takes intangible concepts and turns them into a tangible, monetized asset. Another is the sale of your business, as documentation is required as part of the due diligence process. I have a friend who sells businesses. He has seen companies sell for a fraction of what they are worth because of inadequate documentation.

And of course, there is legal, too. Good documentation protects you if you are sued (and lawyers aren't cheap).

But don't let legal or other obvious documents overpower the broader conversation you should be having about documentation. There are many less apparent areas that are more compelling and where documentation has the potential to increase value.

Projects are expensive, and the main expense for organizations is time— of staff, managers, leadership, accountants, IT support, consultants, and other third parties. Your organization owns that time they spend. I am not implying that you need micromanagement or rigid control over your people. To squeeze ROI from that stiff price tag, there's a better way—documentation. This could be documentation of how the system is built, how the processes are designed, why decisions were made, notes taken from key meetings, the thinking behind why something wasn't done, key insights that were uncov-ered, or how those new processes were impacted.

In my own business, documentation of meeting notes and what my team is thinking translates immediately to client deliverables (that means *money*). If I lose those notes, I need to redo the work—it costs me time.

Other areas where documentation increases your organization's value include:

- **Smarter business processes:** Your company's processes create a system that allows repeatability and scale. This means growth and expansion to take on more customers and products.
- **Marketing clout:** Your brand, messaging, and customer communications—cemented through documentation—are assets to be managed and protected. Your brochures, your proposal mate-rials, and your blogs expand your presence.
- **Consultant ROI:** You can pay big money for consultants with expertise, experience, and wisdom, but without documentation like written reports, presentations, and organized, accessible files, you will watch all that advice (and the fees you paid for it) walk right out the door. Documentation stretches your consulting dollar.
- **Optimized human capital:** Training materials help your people do their jobs better, faster, consistently, safely, and accurately. Docu-mentation lets you get more people up and running quickly.
- **Time saving:** Documentation takes the pressure off your time. In my own business, relying on short written updates and going into my team's files saves me hours a day in update meetings. This gives me time back for doing more meaningful work or seeing my kids once in a while.

Capture the Collective Brain—Getting Intelligence on Paper

The sum of documentation is greater than your organization's individual parts. Your investment in hiring and training employees and bringing in contractors and consultants has generated a collective framework unique to your organization. Your organization owns the value created by the synergies of the people you have brought together.

Documentation lets you capture these synergies and store them in a system where intellectual capital can be retrieved and unlocked for your own competitive advantage. This includes:

- **Intellectual Capital:** Information in the heads of your organization's employees and consultants
- **Intellectual Property:** Information from your organization's employees and consultants that has been effectively captured into tangible documentation, becoming an asset (like a patent or copyright)

Use Dynamic Documentation to leverage your intellectual capital and property. Most organizations spend tons of money finding, training, and retaining the best employees and pumping out fees for consultants and contractors to provide new expertise. While this cycle of hiring, training, and consulting is a normal part of business, without a smart documentation system, your organization becomes an idea sieve. You will lose the ideas, processes, and systems developed during this cycle if a situation (or employee) changes. You are then stuck "reinventing the wheel."

Your organization faces tremendous risk associated with the loss of information locked inside the heads of employees and contractors. In our knowledge-based economy, it is a risk that intensifies with each passing year, as people change jobs more frequently and as layoff and retirement rates increase. You need to take a deliberate and consistent approach to capturing the knowledge of your people.

This means both Big D programs and Little d practices working together (e.g., documenting job functions; technical knowledge of processes, systems, and infrastructure; and capturing the content and creativity that is not yet a formal part of your organization).

Without documentation, you are putting your company at a higher risk of losing knowledge and functionality, resulting in considerable rework— and a loss of both time and money.

Communicate and Connect—Getting People on the Same Page

Solving your documentation problem when working with other departments may feel like toppling the Tower of Babel. Too many information silos. Too much territoriality.

Professions like accounting, law, and engineering are built on hundreds of years of history and have their own languages for talking about documentation. Even newer professions like sales, IT, and Information Management have their own dialects, too.

Professionals are comfortable with their own. Lawyers want to write like lawyers. Accountants talk control and backup. Engineers need insane accuracy (which is good for keeping our airplanes in the air). But these silos make it challenging when you need them to work together. Dynamic Documentation is a decoder for these diverse languages. It offers common best practices for all disciplines and departments.

Dynamic Documentation is a progressive way of training our professionals on documentation. In my CPA articling, my documentation training was literally "the audit step says this" or "fill in this template." I developed severe docu-phobia as result, an ailment that has taken me years to overcome. From my conversations with engineer and lawyer friends, their experience is the same. Documentation was jammed down their throats with little explanation of why it matters and how it makes people better at their work.

Dynamic Documentation will help new, junior professionals (whether you are a CPA, lawyer, engineer, salesperson, or analyst) in all industries to have a common ground for training.

Dynamic Documentation compels people—of all professions, departments, and industries—to spell out what they are thinking. No matter how much we may want to believe everyone is "on the same page," relying on verbal conversations does not get you far, and many times can burn you (something I've learned from experience).

Don't assume everyone is on the same page. This took me years to fully understand and accept. When I started my career, I assumed I was the only one in the meeting who didn't quite get what went on. Over the years, I have come to realize most people—even senior people—leave meetings without understanding what was said or expected in terms of next steps. Unfortunately, corporate culture allows this. We don't understand what just went on and we rarely do anything about it. Managers are not clear and pass this problem along to their staff. Too many of us are stuck in cultures founded on lack of clarity.

Documentation challenges us to be clearer with ourselves and others. Actually, it demands it. Documentation eliminates misunderstandings, misinterpretations, or omitted action items. It drives you to understanding.

THE 6 STEPS OF DYNAMIC DOCUMENTATION

Now, let me finally introduce you to the 6 Steps of Dynamic Documentation. This is the core of this book and the entire focus of part two.

Dynamic Documentation is much more than the documents themselves or the systems that store and organize them. It's a powerful cycle that connects your tangible documents to a larger process and much larger picture. To connect with this picture, you need to learn the skills, techniques, and "secrets" within each of the 6 Steps.

Step 1. Capturing

Capturing is about getting information out of someone's head and onto paper through an interview, note-taking in a meeting or at a conference, or pulling information out of a tool or technology. The point is that you need the information in front of you in some form to start Dynamic Documentation.

Step 2. Structuring

Structuring is the ability to "do something" with the information you have captured. This means the ability to create a document, a set of documents, or a system by shaping the information you have.

Step 3. Presenting

Presenting is about writing and using visual techniques to improve the clarity, effectiveness, and engagement of your documents. If your documents are dry as toast, your people are far more likely to move on to more interesting things.

Step 4. Communicating

Communicating is about getting your message out there to the people who need it. Communicating is a two-way street. It is about capturing feedback, building rapport, and driving meaningful conversation and connection.

Step 5. Storing and Leveraging

Storing and Leveraging is about making your information easy to find by storing it in the right place (usually a system or folder structure), and then leveraging (using, engaging with, updating) this valuable information over time.

Step 6. Leading and Innovating

Dynamic Documentation is about being a "doer-leader" who empowers decision-makers and makes action and improvement contagious throughout their organization. Leaders use documentation practices to drive change and to shape and create the future.

We will get into the detail on the 6 Steps of Dynamic Documentation and the skills to develop for each step in part two. But first let's take a hard look at the documentation problem that you—or your team, department, or organization—is trying to solve. I will show you some tools for assessing where your documentation is, how to spot and frame your challenges, and what to do next.

CHAPTER 2

Where Are You
and How Can You
Get Started?

*Intentions don't
solve problems;
skilled and
consistent
actions do.*

T o make documentation meaningful—and even urgent—so it helps you
in the here and now, you need to look at the reality of your situation and
that of your team, department, or organization. What problem, recurring frustration, or crisis are you facing? What exactly is eating you at work?
Is there something burning that you need to attack immediately?

Once we get more specific about what's not working (problems) we need
to take stock and audit our level of documentation (benchmarks), the quality
of the documentation we have (standards), and the talent we have (skills).

WHAT'S YOUR DOCUMENTATION PROBLEM?

To name a few possibilities:

- Your department spends an inordinate amount of time looking for
  information.
- You are in charge of a new team and are starting from scratch.
- Your team has great ideas, but no one ever follows up.
- You are stuck in a vortex of meetings.

- Your business depends on strong processes, but few, if any, are written down.
- Sally is the only person who knows how to run a critical process in your company.
- Peter built your critical systems from scratch fifteen years ago and is retiring in two months.
- You implemented a fancy document system but haven't seen any results.
- You hired a top consulting firm but haven't seen any results.
- Your company is faced with regulatory and compliance audits.
- Your company is going public next year.
- Your sales are skyrocketing, and your business needs to "grow up" quickly.
- Your company is constantly chasing new "transformation" projects with lots of hype, flashy presentations, big meetings, and the same subpar results.
- You are pulling your hair out trying to get your team to document.

Your documentation problem (e.g., messy files, documentation system implementation) might be obvious. Or it might be *not so obvious* (e.g., dropping the ball). It could be a Big D issue (e.g., new division, regulatory audit) or a Little d issue (e.g., meetings with no outcomes).

No matter the issue, every time you are faced with a problem at work, you can use documentation to work through it. Let's take a look at some of the specific categories your "documentation problem" may fall into . . .

Big D documentation issues:
- Audit findings
- Regulatory issues or risks
- Compliance requirements
- Lack of documentation to support processes or systems
- No written processes or procedures
- Stalled decision-making, launches, pitches
- Failed system implementation

Little d documentation issues:
- Inability to execute on ideas
- Information "locked" in people's heads
- Ineffective meetings
- Losing sales opportunities
- Inability to make timely decisions
- Poor follow-up

Documentation opportunities:
- New company
- New business line or division
- New project or business case
- New system
- New people
- New process or practices

YOUR DYNAMIC DOCUMENTATION PHILOSOPHY

Before you jump into solving your problem, consider how you, your team, or your organization sees documentation. When you hear "documentation," what comes to mind?

Are you and your colleagues docu-phobic? Or docu-zealots? Take a moment to think about your documentation philosophy.

Next, think about where your organization sits on the spectrum—are you leading or bleeding edge, or are you traditionalists?

The breakthrough companies that propel the world forward have a distinct ability to harness intellectual capital and execute on it. They may not always call this process "documentation," but that is exactly what they're doing—capturing and ultimately executing on information.

When Facebook is documenting your preferences as you click "like" on a trending article that catches your attention, it's capturing and storing this information about you for later retrieval so it can more effectively target its ads and show you more of what you like or what's relevant to you. Targeted ads mean more clicks, and more clicks mean more ad revenue and more potential sales for the businesses paying for those specialized ads. All that is made possible thanks to data documentation and a company prepared to use and execute on that stored documentation.

Remember the names of the world's top companies in 2008? They included Exxon Mobil, General Electric, AT&T, and Procter & Gamble. While these product-based companies are still top performers, they have been usurped in market cap by data-driven companies like Apple, Google, and Amazon (with Microsoft remaining at the top, in second after Apple).

Data-driven companies shooting for world domination status are doing something right when it comes to documentation. Yes, they employ the most modern technology and top-of-the-line marketing, but their foundation is mastery of information and documentation, amplified through technology and speed. They capture information and transform it into intellectual capital and then into *money*! This is a sign of a remarkable documentation process.

But wait, you say, we can't *all* be Amazons. I get it. Reading books and going to conferences that talk about Amazon, Google, and Facebook can be inspiring, but may leave us feeling a bit dissatisfied and discouraged. Let's face it, Jeff Bezos's story is not reflective of most businesses, entrepreneurs, or the average employee on their career journey.

The Amazons of the world have tremendous brains, talent, and are backed by throngs of investors. Because of their successes and access to the market, they have colossal (seemingly unlimited) resources. I want to make what I have learned about the documentation philosophies that "get it" digestible to everyone else and their career, life, and business journey—not just the Amazons.

But how can you apply documentation to your "normal" business, department, or team and still skyrocket results?

Dynamic companies, departments, teams, or people have a Dynamic Documentation philosophy. You don't need to be Amazon to have one, either. You just need a mantra that describes how you approach documentation or information as a whole.

Your company (or team or department, for that matter) probably has a documentation philosophy already, but you don't know what it is because it's not codified. Your philosophy may be "do as little as possible" or "don't fail the audit" or "document enough to stay out of jail." And, yes, emails are discoverable.

But these are not inspiring philosophies, which is why documentation is not exactly exciting you and your staff.

Here's what it takes to have the right documentation philosophy, based on my experience working with many companies, departments, and teams over the years:

- Management is genuinely interested in documentation.
- There is a focus on using documentation concepts to drive action.
- There is recognition that documentation should be high quality.
- There is an understanding that documentation must be shareable, usable, and practical.
- There's an understanding that documentation is not created for documentation's sake.
- The organization uses lean (that is, iterative and "good enough") documentation techniques.

My personal documentation philosophy is to use it as my superpower. Every company, team, or department needs its own philosophy, which will evolve over time. If you are a rapidly growing business, your documentation philosophy may be about scale. If you are an established department, your documentation philosophy might be about efficiency and communication across departments. If your team sells innovative products, your documentation philosophy may be about accelerated speed to market. If you are a small business owner, your documentation philosophy may be about fostering peace of mind.

Take a moment while this is all fresh in your mind and ask yourself:

- What is your personal documentation philosophy?
- What is your company's (or team's or department's) philosophy?
- How are these philosophies serving you? Limiting you?
- How could you change your philosophy to serve you better?

YOUR DOCUMENTATION AUDIT: BENCHMARKS FOR THE 5 STAGES OF DOCUMENTATION

Before we jump into solving your problem, let's see which stage you're in. Think of this as a documentation audit, or "stress test."

While it isn't as technical as other standards in the information governance space (like the ISO 23081 records management processes), the Dynamic Documentation benchmarks approach is a quick, do-it-yourself way of measuring the maturity of your documentation. Identifying your primary stage will give you an idea of how to attack the documentation problem in front of you and where you need to go next.

There are five distinct stages that organizations, departments, projects, or teams tend to fall into:

Stages of Documentation

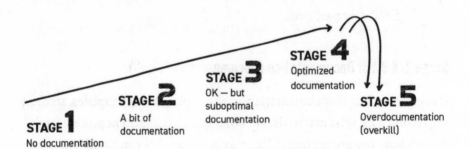

- **Stage 1.** No Documentation (Blank Slate)
- **Stage 2.** A Bit of Documentation (Documentation "Lite")
- **Stage 3.** OK, but Suboptimal Documentation ("Check-the-Box")
- **Stage 4.** Optimized Documentation (Just-Right Documentation)
- **Stage 5.** Overdocumentation (Overkill)

Stage 1. No Documentation (Blank Slate)

If you are a new company or have just been put in charge of a new business line, project, or team, you are in Stage 1.

Stage 1s have a lot of work to do. But they also have the advantage of starting from a clean slate. You can use the full suite of Dynamic Documentation skills and tips to develop your documentation or work through your challenges. You can also begin with your own practice and your work with colleagues to get on the same page, sustain momentum, and develop checklists, as well as take better notes and design simple templates and systems that will free up time and attention for bigger things. Now that you are reading this book, you are off to the races.

What are signs of Stage 1?
- No documentation, systems, or processes—a blank slate!

Next steps?
- Set your documentation philosophy.
- Define a few documentation objectives for the next month and quarter.
- Work through the 6 Steps of Dynamic Documentation from start to finish (see part two).

Stage 2. A Bit of Documentation (Documentation "Lite")

If you have a "bit" of documentation, such as some forms, templates, accounting records, and sales materials, but not much of a consistent process for documentation, you are in Stage 2. You may be a Stage 2 if you have lots of notes, but you don't have a process yet for getting value out of them.

There is a good chance you are in Stage 2 if you are a private company, entrepreneur, or personal business owner, but organizations aren't precluded from this stage. I have worked with government bodies and public companies—including segments of large multinationals—that are stuck in Stage 2 as well.

Many Stage 2s scrape by until there is a burning, immediate challenge (e.g., lawsuit, going public, retirement of a key employee, regulatory requirement, loss of critical information, or embarrassment with a customer or a boss) to push them up to the next stage. If you work in a Stage 2 environment and don't want to wait for that burning platform to collapse out from under you, you will need formalize and practice the 6 Steps of Dynamic Documentation in your own sphere and sell others on why Dynamic Documentation matters.

What are signs of Stage 2?
- Little or sporadic documentation
- No documentation systems or codification
- Minimal processes in place
- Few meeting notes, sales records, communications, and unresolved culture around documentation

Next steps?
- Sell your team on why organization-wide Dynamic Documentation matters.
- Define your current documentation philosophy and what you'd like your future philosophy to be.
- Work through the 6 Steps of Dynamic Documentation, focusing on the missing parts of your documentation program.

Stage 3. OK but Suboptimal Documentation ("Check-the-Box")

Most of my clients (at least when I start working with them) are in Stage 3. Many of you reading this book, especially if you come from a large corporate environment, are probably in Stage 3, too.

If you are in Stage 3, you probably have many superficial aspects of documentation in place (e.g., templates, memos, procedures, systems), but your documentation and related practices are not working as well as they should.

If your team or your company is in Stage 3, you may be "going through the motions" when it comes to documentation. You are "doing" but not "getting" documentation.

You are probably documenting what is obvious to satisfy your customers, suppliers, auditors, and regulators. But your team doesn't recognize the connection between documentation and improving behavior, driving action, and paving the road to success.

Many Stage 3s believe they are Stage 4s. "We have lots of documentation around XYZ process!" Stage 3s take a checklist approach—they believe that just "having documentation" is enough. If that is your company, documentation may be giving you a false sense of security and you are missing out on the returns a topflight effort would deliver.

Stage 3s typically understand the role of Information Management (information) and the Organizational Design (process) in documentation, but they completely miss the Personal Productivity (people) circle of the Documentation Triad.

You need *people* to make documentation work. Metamorphic change doesn't come from tidying your files or metadata; it comes from reforming how your people engage with information in their day-to-day work.

Without a conscious and deliberate effort to invest in documentation, Stage 3 is where most organizations and teams will live indefinitely. Dynamic Documentation will teach you to propel yourself into Stage 4.

Although you may not need to sell your company on doing documentation in the first place (as in Stage 2), you may need to sell them on the value of documentation beyond just "because of the audit" or "because the boss said so."

What are signs of Stage 3?
- Documentation in place but little connection to its value
- Weak or sporadic documentation of processes or meetings
- Reactive, not proactive, documentation
- Issues that are talked about in circles and never reach a solution
- Lack of momentum on projects
- Failure to realize potential of staff members or consultants
- Documents that aren't read or referenced
- Documents and document systems that don't resonate with your staff

Next steps?
- Define your documentation philosophy and where you want to take it.
- Align your philosophy with your company's goals.

- Take an inventory of what documents, systems, and supporting processes you have.
- Take an inventory of the skills of your team.
- Work through the 6 Steps of Dynamic Documentation, focusing on your weakest areas.
- Align Little d and Big D concepts, and get Little d up to par.

Stage 4. Optimized Documentation (Just-Right Documentation)

Stage 4 is the "ideal" to which you should aspire in your documentation journey. At this level, management regularly reviews and rewards strong documentation. There are established routines around documentation and, most importantly, your documentation is being used.

So, how can you move from Stage 3 to Stage 4? The leap isn't like quite like a movie montage where the music turns and your team goes from hating documentation to loving it overnight. The shift can be subtle. But it can, like magic, also happen quickly.

There isn't one path that moves you from Stage 3 to Stage 4. It depends on what your team or organization needs and what obstacles you are facing. My experience is that these stumbling blocks are often not as high as they seem. You can get over them through simple but effective documentation techniques.

Some examples from my own experience in moving clients from Stage 3 to 4 include building a portal to access information, implementing a reporting practice for a compliance program, and using interviews to speed up a project. Moving to Stage 4 has nothing to do with being "perfect" either. You know that you're there when documentation is improving how people work.

If you are part of a large organization and are in Stage 4, it's doubtful other departments and divisions within your company are all up there with you. You can still work through the 6 Steps of Dynamic Documentation to become a "Super Stage 4"!

Use your processes, techniques, and results to promote Dynamic Documentation across your organization and broaden its applications to other teams, departments, projects, and applications. Dynamic Documentation is contagious, and its gospel will spread.

What are signs of Stage 4?
- "Fit for purpose" documentation
- Proactive documentation practices
- Usable, practical documentation systems and tools
- Consistent meeting notes to capture ideas and actions
- Documentation that is used, communicated, and talked about
- Regular documentation updates

Next steps?
- Focus on what is working and write it down—tell a good news story to others in your company.
- Leverage your institutional knowledge, systems, processes, and practices for other teams in your company.
- In reviewing the 6 Steps of Dynamic Documentation, pay special attention to the "Storing and Leveraging" (Step 5) and the "Leading and Innovating" (Step 6) chapters to understand how to maintain your documentation and improve it continuously in the long run.

Stage 5. Overdocumentation (Overkill)

If you are drowning in documentation and related systems and practices, you have the opposite problem of Stages 1 and 2. You could call Stage 5 the overkill stage. It is the most expensive of all the stages, and sometimes the most dangerous. And it's also very common.

Unfortunately, in the documentation world, we tend to swing to extremes—either barely any documentation or mountains of it. Stage 5s are found in organizations where there is fear of failing regulatory requirements (e.g., SOX, the Sarbanes-Oxley Act of 2002), a lack of ability to write and communicate succinctly, or a lack of understanding of what information users and the company really need.

And many documentation specialists love detail, which gives us a personality bias toward overdocumentation, too.

Maybe you are in Stage 5 because you had a consultant who dumped every complicated "best practice" on your department, or maybe you had a business analyst who documented every little detail, or an IT vendor who sold you a Ferrari when you needed a bicycle. These are not uncommon scenarios.

As a Canadian with lots of experience in the oil and gas sector—where times can be very good and then very bad—I have seen Stage 5 projects creep up especially when times are good and companies have more resources and money to burn on grand ideas. This often results in too much money spent, too many committees formed, and too little movement forward. Ironically, it is often easier to work with clients when times are leaner and companies are more careful and practical with their documentation resources.

Stage 5s are unfortunately some of the hardest projects to turn around. You must weed through lots of documents, bloated teams, painful templates, and overlapping systems—many of which need a complete overhaul. It is hard to tell an executive that their lengthy documentation or "best-in-class" system is not what they need. We feel attached to the projects we sponsor, and it's hard to let go. (Researchers call this the IKEA effect, where we admire the bookshelf we built ourselves more than another bookshelf, even if it's a bit off-kilter.)

If you are in Stage 5, Dynamic Documentation will help you to shed the fat with "lean" thinking to make your documentation practices digestible, functional, cost effective, and smart.

What are signs of Stage 5?
- Overthinking and redoing documentation
- Documents that are never "good enough" or just never seem to reach completion
- Complex documentation storage systems, workflows, templates, and metadata
- Excessively long documents
- Unreasonable documentation policies or standards

- Endless review and edit cycles
- More work on documentation than value coming out

Next steps?
- Work through the 6 Steps of Dynamic Documentation and look for places where you can apply lean thinking.
- Focus your documentation efforts on where you want to go (not what documentation you have already).
- Assess how you can get your team to unlearn bad documentation practices.

With this 5-Stage benchmark laid out, if you haven't already, ask yourself:

- Which stage does your team, project, department, or organization fall into?
- Which one do you fall into personally—in different areas of your life (work, home, personal projects, administration)?

Be honest. Dynamic Documentation is about getting your team, your project, your company, and your individual processes to Stage 4—and staying there for good.

THE 5 SUPER STANDARDS—A NEW MODEL TO MEASURE YOUR DOCUMENTATION

Now that you know which stage you are in, you can diagnose your documentation problem from another angle.

The 5 Super Standards—Re-Performance, Clarity, Findability, Use, and Engagement—will give you insight into what is working, what is not working, and the sources of your documentation problems. Use these standards to judge your documentation and focus your energy on the right areas.

The Re-Performance Standard

Re-Performance Standard: The ability of a stand-alone document or system to allow a user to perform the related task or process *again*.

I think of the Re-Performance Standard as a best-kept secret of the audit world. Auditors probably don't want to share it because the rule is so effective that it might make audits irrelevant. I swear by this standard for audits and Internal Control work. It is the standard adopted by the Big Four accounting firms and by professional accounting and audit bodies. It is the world's de facto standard for Internal Controls over Financial Reporting (ICFR).

When I work with companies beyond their audit or accounting needs, I apply this concept to achieve the same powerful results in areas such as:

- **Training materials:** Can the user perform his or her job using the documentation? Is it easy for a new employee to get up to speed?
- **User manuals:** Does the user understand the application or system? Does the documentation help employees use the system?
- **Process documentation:** Can the user perform the process following the documentation? Does it describe the process in enough detail?
- **Disaster recovery documentation:** Does the user know what to do in the case of a disaster? Can a user carry out the steps successfully in the case of an emergency?
- **Safety documentation:** Can the user understand the process clearly enough to prevent an incident? Can the user re-perform all safety procedures?
- **Marketing documentation:** Can the sales team deliver a consistent message to clients? Can the sales team find materials easily to execute on opportunities quickly?

Let's look at this simple example to take a better look at the Re-Performance Standard.

How to get to the Calgary Airport from the Bow Valley Square building (without the Re-Performance Standard)

Getting to the airport involves going on Deerfoot, 96 Ave. NE, Memorial, and Airport Road. The trip takes 21 minutes. The route involves a turn on Deerfoot after Memorial and then the route goes to 96 Ave. You need to get on 5 Ave. SW first. It is important to note that Airport Trail merges into 96 Ave. before you hit the airport.

What do you think, could you get to the Calgary Airport with these instructions?

Here are the directions that meet the Re-Performance Standard (pulled from Google Maps, which relies on the Re-Performance Standard)

1. Head east on 5 Ave. SW toward 1 St. SW (750 m)
2. Continue straight onto 5 Ave. SE N (400 m)
3. Use the right two lanes to turn right onto Memorial Dr. (2.4 km)
4. Use the right lane to take the ramp onto Deerfoot Trail North (600 m)
5. Take exit 266 at 96 Ave. NE/Airport Trail NE E (11.4 km)
6. Keep right at the fork, follow signs for Airport Tr./Airport and merge onto 96 Ave NE/Airport Trail NE E (1 km)
7. Turn right onto Barlow Trail (800 m)
8. Turn right onto Airport Rd. NE (650 m)

The Re-Performance Standard means that you need enough detail for the next user to understand you. But too much detail has the opposite effect.

Now look at what happens when we take the example above and then change it to add too much detail (overcorrecting the original problem of lack of detail).

How to get to the Calgary Airport (adding too much detail)

1. Head east on 5 Ave. SW toward 1 St. SW (750 m) where you will see the Suncor Energy Centre East Tower (formerly the Petro-Canada Centre). This is

an 181,000 square meter (1,945,000 square foot) project composed of two granite and reflective glass-clad office towers of thirty-two floors and fifty-two floors. Planning for the complex began in the late 1970s following the creation of Petro-Canada. (Yes, I googled this.)

Need I say more? You get the picture.

Clarity Standard

Clarity Standard: The ability of the stand-alone document to clearly explain the intended use of the document to the intended audience.

The Clarity Standard is something you probably do instinctively. While it seems like a no-brainer, it is shocking how often the Clarity Standard isn't followed. How many resumes or LinkedIn profiles have you read and wondered what this "results-oriented people-person" actually does?

You can test your documentation using the Clarity Standard by asking:

- Does the reader understand the document without someone explaining it?
- Are the key concepts "getting through" to the reader?
- Are the key concepts understood by the reader quickly?
- Are there any gaps in the reader's understanding?
- Does the reader understand the message easily?
- Does it support the Business Judgment Rule (i.e., the legal standard which assesses whether management can prove they did their due diligence)?

Findability Standard

Findability Standard: The ability to easily and quickly find a document or other piece of information using the stand-alone system, setup, or process.

Search and findability functions are what many of your users will see as the main drivers of your documentation project or program, especially if you are designing systems and sites. Your users will want to be able to find things quickly with as little thinking as possible.

The master of the Findability Standard is Google, which has perfected the standard and spoiled us in doing so. Most people believe information should be as easy to find as it is to google.

But behind what seems like Google's simple search function is world-class technology and thousands of highly paid programmers and software engineers. Google is drawing from a *massive* amount of information, which improves the results you get back. Meeting the Findability Standard is not as easy as googling!

You can test your documentation systems for the findability standard by asking:

- Can a user find documentation without asking others?
- Can team members find documentation quickly?
- Does the team or organization know what documentation it has?
- Does the team have criteria around what are critical documents, how they are named, and where they are stored?

Use Standard

Use Standard: The frequency of use of your documents or document systems.

I have built beautiful web pages for projects that no one has looked at. I have put together thoroughly designed processes that no one has looked at. I have built documentation storage systems and found out later that people are just working off their personal drives.

The Use Standard asks if your audience is looking at the documents you created.

- Did anyone use the document or documentation system after it was developed?
- Is the documentation used going forward? How often?
- Is anyone asking questions about the documents or engaging with its content?
- Is anyone referencing the documents or documentation systems?

Engagement Standard

Engagement Standard: A measurement of whether the user was able to grasp the key concepts quickly and efficiently, and their ability to recall the messages and information in the document.

The Engagement Standard could also be called the "sticky" standard. You know your document is meeting the Engagement Standard when you get any of the following:

- **Recollection:** You hear points from your document talked about in a meeting.
- **Impact:** You see the recommendations or ideas in your document being implemented.
- **Reaction:** You get questions or feedback about your documents (even corrections or criticisms).
- **Thinking:** Your document impacts decision-making.
- **Emotion:** Your document makes people excited, energized, or concerned.

When you hear your document, report, or analysis brought up in meetings or other conversations, you know it was successful. This may be a reflection of the Use Standard (whether it was a good idea, well communicated) and it may also be a reflection of the Engagement Standard (whether the document and the related points were *sticky*). Engagement and the Use Standard go hand in hand. If your stuff is not engaging, it probably won't get used.

But assume for a moment that someone did see your materials (even briefly, like by email or when you presented it in a meeting). If your materials are not sticking and no one can recall what was written, you probably have an engagement problem. Our ability to make things stick in the minds of our audience tests our Little d intuition and a combination of skills that we will get into later in this book.

As you think about these measures, consider how your documents, processes, and systems line up to the standards. Consider which ones are most

Super Standards

STANDARD	POTENTIAL CAUSES OF ISSUES
Re-Performance Standard	• Poor writing skills or ability to communicate clearly • Weak document review cycle • Lack of understanding of the material being written • Missing or incomplete information • Missing or lack of processes, procedures, manuals, and training guides • Excessive, irrelevant details
Clarity Standard	• Lack of clear purpose • Poor technical writing skills • No visual aids or weak layout and design • Weak review or feedback cycle • Audience is not well understood • Too much information
Findability Standard	• Weak folder structure • Too many garbage documents • Poorly designed systems, workflows, or metadata, or lack thereof • Failure to separate work in progress and archived documents • Lack of regular cleanup of documents • No accountability over existing documents and systems
Use Standard	• A bad idea for your document, system, or process in the first place • Lack of communication of the documentation or system • Team members don't like your documents • Team members don't have a documentation mindset • Weak writing or visual design skills
Engagement Standard	• Lack of understanding of human psychology • Lack of personality (energy, emotion, humor) in your documentation • Academic or jargony writing style • Lack of understanding of dynamic writing • Lack of dynamic design

applicable to your situation and what these standards tell you about your documentation problem. Reference this table to understand the issues you may be facing.

WHAT IS YOUR DOCUMENTATION "SKILL STACK"?

No matter which stage you're in or which of the 5 Super Standards you're meeting (or not), moving your documentation forward will always come back to people. People will solve your documentation problem, not your systems or your documents themselves. More specifically, people with the right documentation skills will. Think about your team, their skills, and what you might be missing.

A "talent stack" is a concept coined by *Dilbert* comic creator Scott Adams. It's the idea that with a unique *combination* of normal talents, you can be extraordinary. Scott Adams refers to his own skills as an example: He has combined a bit of business knowledge, drawing skills, and humor with a strong work ethic to build a world-famous comic series.

While I agree with stacking talent when it comes to documentation, I also know that no one is born knowing how to document, and no one has— or needs to have—all the talents needed to move work forward. We can strengthen our effectiveness by building our individual skills and joining forces with others.

Dynamic Documentation is much more of a "skill" stack than a "talent" stack. This means you need to build a full repertoire of documentation skills. Combined, these skills become a powerful force. Thus, the first "secret" of Dynamic Documentation:

➡ The Skill Stack Solution ➡

tells us to identify the specific documentation skills for each project or task and to identify our own skills and those of our team—and to build and source additional skills as necessary.

Dynamic Documentation Skill Stack

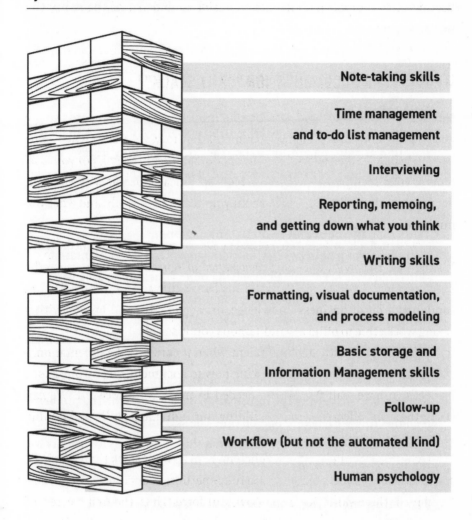

Note-taking skills

Time management
and to-do list management

Interviewing

Reporting, memoing,
and getting down what you think

Writing skills

Formatting, visual documentation,
and process modeling

Basic storage and
Information Management skills

Follow-up

Workflow (but not the automated kind)

Human psychology

You can "stack" your skills and those of your team for Dynamic Documentation. For example, if you are an IT professional, but you happen to be an excellent writer (a rare combination, I might add), you can "stack" these talents to create IT documentation that puts you leagues ahead of your teammates. Or, you might be exceptionally gifted at visual design techniques. In this case, stack your talents with a partner who is a genius at organizing complex ideas, and design documentation systems that are attractive and useful. Apply the skill stack to your team and combine an idea person with a follow-upper to reach your goals.

Here are the key documentation skills that you should hire and train for in your team:

Note-taking skills

You need skills on your team for getting notes, information, and materials into or onto something to start the documentation process. While note-taking may seem straightforward, it is surprising how few people do it well.

Time management and to-do list management

There is a strong tie between time management and documentation skills that have been applied to getting more done. Organizing your work, project, or team depends on a foundation of capturing and structuring your to-dos and planning how and when to do them.

Interviewing

In my years of developing thousands of documents, hands down the best approach to getting the information we need and solving problems is connecting with people one-on-one. The skill of listening without an agenda and getting others to share what they know leads to insights we can't get any other way.

Reporting, memoing, and getting down what you think

Dynamic reporting has nothing to do with being a good writer. It is about getting more out of your brain and onto paper. You have a lot to share. So do your team members. But we all need the skill of getting what we know and think captured somewhere to make it usable to ourselves and to others.

Writing skills

Your team needs writing skills for Dynamic Documentation. This one's a nonstarter. Writing skills are the ability to get things on paper in the first place (and quickly) and the ability to be clear, practical, and engaging.

Formatting, visual documentation, and process modeling
Stack your team or get access to resources with visual or graphical skills to make your documents pop. Visual techniques such as layout, design, diagramming, and process modeling are essential for great documentation.

Basic storage and Information Management skills
While you might not need an Information Management or information governance expert on your team, basic storage and Information Management skills are key. Managing information is everyone's job. Your team should understand the principles of file structure, document workflow, metadata, and basic storage systems (e.g., SharePoint and Dropbox for Business).

Follow-up
Dynamic Documentation is a lot like sales, but your "sale" is getting your idea or initiative across, often inside a company. Like a great salesperson, this means you have the superpower to get people to make decisions, act, and execute on your new process, improvement, plan, or solution. Follow-up is an underrated grit skill.

Workflow (but not the automated kind)
In our knowledge-based economy, we are all walking information processors. Our skill of managing the information that comes into our day is an art, science, and practice that is very personal (and very Little d). You will soon learn about the 24-Hour Rule and other secrets and tips for improving your personal workflow, whether through your emails, notes, files, communications, meetings, or other means.

Human psychology
Dynamic Documentation requires intuition into knowing what people want to see and hear. You can be "right" all you want about how lousy

the new point-of-sale system is, but you need tact to write a memo to communicate the deficiencies to your boss. Your team can pump out the strongest reports and repositories, but they will be useless without a connection with your audience. Documentation demands an understanding of what makes people tick and how they connect with information. Understanding human psychology is where your smarts shine through.

With your new understanding of the superpower of documentation, let's get into the actual 6 Steps of Dynamic Documentation. Think of the multi-tiered approach as a cable with entwined strands. The combination of specific skills and habits will be transformative. And you'll have more fun, too, through the process.

PART
2

The 6 Steps of Dynamic Documentation

CHAPTER 3

—

Capturing

If you want to remember it, document it.

C apturing is where the Dynamic Documentation process starts. Think of it as mining for gold, digging for buried treasure, sleuthing for clues, hunting for prey, diving for pearls (or whatever floats your boat or turns your crank).

For some of us, the Capturing phase creates anxiety. Will documenting ideas somehow result in criticism? Will it negatively impact career growth? Maybe it's better to just "sleep on it" and see how it plays in the morning?

And the reality is: Finding your best pieces of information is a lot like hitting a baseball. You try your best and sometimes you fail. In the world of major league baseball, a batting average of .300 or better is the mark of a top-tier hitter. That means, you understand, that this player will fail to get a hit seven out of ten times.

So please capture those nuggets and cultivate ideation. And document, document, document. The pursuit of excellence will sometimes result in a "strike out," and that's OK.

The prize you are looking for may come from your own head, someone else's head, a team meeting, a brainstorming session, a webinar, something you heard on the news, or a conversation around the water cooler. Whatever your source, you need a system—and a habit—for trapping this information so it doesn't escape. From there, you will tame, train, and polish it to make the magic happen.

Organizations that are capturing-challenged often have:

- Too many meetings
- A bounty of ideas but no follow-through
- A need to re-explain or retrain people frequently

Capturing problems often go undetected in organizations. Like toxic fumes that you can't smell, they are deadly. If your team can't capture ideas, concepts, materials, and feedback, your Big D projects (e.g., process design, policy initiative, governance program) are stuck in the mud. Your team needs the Little d skills of listening, interviewing, and note-taking to have a fighting chance.

Why is capturing so difficult? There are a few human biases that get in our way. The first is that, because knowledge is power, it's a form of currency. We are often reluctant to share what we know—our currency—and the same goes for our colleagues. Another is that we are afraid of being wrong. Looking stupid is one of our deepest human fears.

But there's another, bigger hurdle. We rely on our short-term memories and fail to capture information that we need. Big mistake. *Not* smart. Our short-term memory stinks. I know what you're saying: "No, not me!" Trust me. Your memory is not as reliable as you think. Though we may like to imagine ourselves as a species of conscientious planners, humans have an optimism bias in this regard. We convince ourselves that we'll remember the gems generated at that last strategy session, but it ain't gonna happen. You know it; I know it.

In the moment, we truly believe we will remember:

- The great idea we heard in a meeting
- The follow-up we need to do that our boss just told us in the hall
- What the issue is with the process we are working through
- What time our appointment is after hanging up from the call to schedule it

- The life-changing tip we hear at a conference, training session, or webinar
- The next steps and decisions the team agreed on in an update call
- The changes to the report that the client requested on the fly
- What we need to pick up for our spouse on our way home from work (yes, this transfers to our personal lives as well)

Our brains are designed by nature to focus on a few key things at a time for our own survival, and remembering the milk just doesn't always make that priority list. Short-term memory is like having Post-it Notes stored at the front of your brain. Your brain doesn't have much prime real estate.

In an influential paper titled "The Magical Number Seven, Plus or Minus Two," psychologist George Miller suggested that people can store between five and nine items in short-term memory. The magic number of items the average adult can hold in short-term memory is seven (plus or minus two), Miller concluded, because of the number of "slots" available.

You only have room for *seven* Post-it Notes. Seven items is not a lot of space for all the Post-it Notes you need for life! At work, you probably have loads more than seven things to get done in your day. More bad news—these Post-it Notes don't always stick. They can easily fall off our brain wall. (Technically, this is when a nerve impulse has stopped transmitting through the neural network; you can look that one up.)

Researchers say that the small capacity of our short-term memory was essential for human survival. We needed to take care of the basics (e.g., keep warm, find food, fend off that saber-toothed tiger) without getting bogged down in the details.

This relatively small short-term memory capacity makes modern-day life difficult. However, when you use Dynamic Documentation skills like writing things down, recapping, or synthesizing, you get this information off your short-term brain wall and into your long-term memory bank. Your long-term memory is like a vault with durable, organized files where information can't "slip" from your mental hard drive.

In this sense, documentation is about training for the long game, because you are adding to this vault every day.

WHERE TO START, WHAT TO CAPTURE

"But, but, but . . ." I hear you saying. I know, we are only human, and it can be tempting to procrastinate on the capturing process. We're more likely to focus on the physical messes in our lives—cleaning our offices, our clothes, our kitchens—rather than the invisible messes and information in our lives.

My recommendation is this: If you have a choice between capturing your information (in a digital or paper form) or cleaning up a physical mess, deal with the information—it will never be there again. Don't procrastinate when it comes to capturing information! *The physical mess will be there tomorrow. The fleeting thoughts will not.*

There are opportunities to capture information all around you, and they appear in many shapes and forms. The key is to be ever-vigilant for these opportunities.

5 Ways to Capture Information

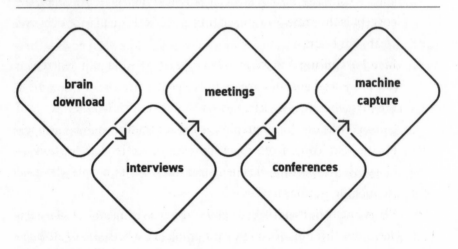

Information Out of Your Own Head: The Brain Download

If you ask me what you as an individual need to do first to improve your documentation, my recommendation for where to start is to capture all the ideas and action items that occur throughout your day.

Our minds are remarkable machines, full of life-changing ideas, thoughts, and potential projects. The problem is they stay stuck in our heads for a time, and then vanish like sandcastles at high tide. I have read that we have seventy thousand thoughts a day. Whether this is apocryphal or not, we know our brains are capturing and sending us thousands of messages a day. Your documentation system needs to capture the pearls so you can do great things with them.

Our minds are also full of to-dos. They pop into our heads before we're out of bed, when we are in meetings, and as we are trying to fall asleep. If you are struggling to harness your to-dos, remember that capturing them is "controlling" them.

Capture all these ideas as soon as possible and put them somewhere. Here are just a few ways you can store them:

- **Journaling:** Even a few minutes of journaling a day can pay huge dividends. Whether you write formally, write in a stream-of-consciousness style, or just jot a few notes down on loose paper, the concept is the same. You are writing to think through a thought and clear your brain.

- **Mind mapping:** A mind map is a type of loose diagram where you place a central goal or concept in the center from which new ideas flow. As a business owner, I use this often to think of new ways of getting business. It is a graphic reminder that my business opportunities can come from many different directions and actions— blogging, prospecting, old clients, existing clients, people who used to work for us, irons in the fire.

- **Blogs and other writing:** Blogs and other writing projects are wonderful for thinking through your problems, whether it is the business problem you are working on or an idea you are just thinking through. Don't worry if you aren't planning on sending the idea to someone; the very process of writing to think can get you a long way.

- **Action items:** Writing down action items is a great way of getting things out of your head. Create a daily list of action items, as well as a running list of items you want to attack over time.

- **Project lists:** Projects are a bit different than action items, which might include things like "send report to Jim." Projects are activities that require several connected activities. You probably have several or more ongoing work, career, personal, and family projects—a report you are working on, a document cleanup exercise, a configuration for the new system, your son's science project, your garage cleanup, planning your summer vacation. Keeping lists helps you keep your projects on track.

A "brain download" (also referred to as "brain dump") is about getting more of the information your brain is holding onto paper. It means that you haven't vetted the thing or subject you are thinking about yet, but you are at least starting the process of transferring your loose thoughts onto paper to find out what you know and what you don't know. It's the best technique for taking stock of what you already know before chasing more information.

Let me give you an example of how effective the brain download is. I was once covering for another auditor. The previous auditor had verbally confirmed that a new procurement system was good to go, and the conclusion looked straightforward. I wanted to do a bit more due diligence given that I was just taking over the file. So, I did a quick brain download of what we knew about the system. As I looked at what had, I thought of a new question we hadn't thought of before. This question ultimately led to our team averting what could have been a significant financial problem. Little d actions (like brain dumps) have Big D results.

Information Out of Someone Else's Head: The Interview Technique

When you are faced with a problem, no matter the scale, one of the best ways to get started is through talking it out.

Rather than relying on trendy approaches used by many consultants (such as workshops, facilitated sessions, surveys, or questionnaires) we can start with something much more basic, personal, and intimate: interviewing. By interviewing, I don't mean for a job, I mean sitting down and talking to someone who has information you need. I mean connecting with someone who runs a function in your company—a coworker, a client, a potential client, a peer, a colleague at another company, a supplier, anyone who might have useful information you can get out of their heads.

Trendier techniques like workshops can yield some good ideas, but, in my professional experience, they are ineffective on their own. Magic happens through the connection between two people.

The Next-Action Interview

Whenever you are stuck on a problem, think about
interviewing someone to get the information, insight,
and inspiration you need to get to the next step.

Interviewing is not an interrogation. It's not a series of rote questions. And it isn't a free-for-all or convo with your bestie either. It's a dynamic dialogue. The best interview questions ask people what they think, as simply put as, "What is working and what is not working?"

Interviews require interpersonal connection that unearths rich information. Through the interview process, you will uncover:

- **Processes and systems:** Often there are processes and systems that are custom-designed, or that only a few people know about, or that are designed by a few individuals over time. I once documented a complex settlement process for a bank that only one employee knew how to run.

- **Unique knowledge:** This refers to issues people know about but that aren't widely shared. Human nature being what it is, many people will share some sensitive issues only when asked in a one-on-one environment. My job as a consultant is often just to put these points on paper and let people be heard.

- **New ideas and suggestions:** I have been given ideas for how to improve countless processes in different contexts through interviewing a client's employees. Many people do not speak up in meetings but will speak up in the intimacy of a trusting interview environment.

- **Roadblocks and momentum-killers**: Private and small-group conversations often get to the heart of projects that are stymied by competing goals, conflicts in management direction, and other issues.

Think of your favorite interviewer. Maybe it's Larry King, Oprah, Jimmy Kimmel, or David Letterman. These people are trained to get to the meat of the issue. They have intuition and charm and know how to flatter their guests to create chemistry and draw out information.

Dynamic interviewing is about doing the same thing. It may sound like a conversation, but it's more than that. Information gushes from your interviewee through a structured and deliberate process. You create chemistry—a shared bond—and ask the right questions. The interviewee is flattered and disarmed, and the information flows.

There is magic in interviewing people—especially those in unsung positions—about their areas, even if it does not seem overly exciting at first. Many of my client interviews are for routine accounting, IT, or administrative processes. I've watched accountants reconcile accounts, schedulers book flights, clerks process payments, and warehouse staff count airplane parts, nuts and bolts, and fish.

Many interviewees love to talk about themselves and even find it therapeutic. Others may want to show off. In the case where the interviewee shuts down (which happens from time to time), and sees the process as an investigation—well, that certainly gives you valuable information, too.

Let me give you an example of how effective interviewing really is. I was working for a large company and was asked to help with an analysis of a complex process required to support a new partnership. There was a group of expensive consultants already working on the problem when I arrived. But their analysis wasn't going very well. The consultants were holding big meetings and spewing out fancy presentations almost daily. I realized what was wrong. They were short-changing (almost entirely skipping) the Capture step of the 6 Steps of Dynamic Documentation.

Over the next three weeks, I moved the project to one-on-one or small-group interviews and away from big meetings and PowerPoint. Our interviews yielded a wealth of information. The answers to our problem were literally sitting in front of us in the heads of our people. By switching to the simpler, unpretentious interview style, we collected more insight, analysis, and ideas in a couple weeks than the consultants had in months.

Information in Meetings: Group Talk and Group Think

The ability to interview is a centerpiece of the capturing process. However, if you ask me what's wrong with most companies' documentation practices, often the issue has nothing to do with their systems or documentation standards; the capturing issue starts with substandard meeting note practices— or the lack of meeting notes altogether. In today's corporate culture, we spend a lot of our days in meetings, whether in person or on Zoom or Teams. But are we really driving action, following up, and gaining momentum from the key findings of these meetings?

Meeting notes are very Little d, but the lack of them quickly escalates to Big D problems, including wasting your people's time, taking wrong actions due to lack of clarity, lack of updates on the project plan, lost intellectual capital, and weak company decisions.

If you have a career in the corporate world, you may spend a good 30 percent of your time in meetings. This could be the equivalent of up to ten years of your life. So, it is worth the effort to learn great meeting habits and turn them into your superpower.

In a meeting, we think, talk, and make decisions as a group. Unlike interviews, meetings are a two-way, three-way, four-way, or more-way style of conversation.

Why do you call your friends up to talk about an issue? Why do you go to therapy? Why do you swing by your coworkers' offices and say, "I just need to think this through"? You want to release the problem into the air using your voice. You want to process the problem with another person.

Most meetings are about group problem-solving. Meetings and the Dynamic Documentation they create are about harnessing the "Can I just talk this through?" conversations. Dynamic meetings and quality note-taking tie back to human psychology and understanding how to capture the magic that emanates from the group dynamic. Documentation practices allow the ideas, emotions, group synergies, and energies from meetings to take wing.

Humans don't think like robots, and we don't talk in a logical order, especially in meetings. We will go around in circles and off on tangents. Even though meetings shouldn't be free-for-alls, they shouldn't be too tightly controlled, either. You wouldn't set an agenda if you called up your best friend to talk through a problem you were having at work. A meeting should strike the right balance between structure and spontaneity.

Capturing practices for dynamic meetings involves:

- **Note-taking:** Note-taking is about capturing ideas, issues, challenges, solutions, and actions discussed during the meeting. Everyone should learn how to take notes. But it's ok to ask a team member to take notes or assign a "scribe" when you need help.
- **Recapping:** Recapping is about writing down and sharing (usually via email) what was heard. Use your note-taking skills and your ability to synthesize to help you, along with strong listening and writing skills.
- **Action items and next steps:** Meetings should prompt additional action items. Capture these next steps and add them to your project plans or follow up on them immediately.
- **Updates to documents:** Your note-taking might involve direct updates to documents, reports, or business cases underway.

Presentations, Conferences, and Other Learning: Your Second Brain

Unlike the insights from interviews and meetings, information captured during presentations and conferences is relatively unambiguous. Presentations and conferences are largely (with the exception of the Q&A process and networking sessions) one-way communications.

I enjoy conferences and presentations, but in my experience, there are only a few tidbits of information from them that truly matter to me. I don't sit there with my head down, taking notes, although I see many attendees doing just that. For some folks, the act of taking unnecessarily copious notes is preferable to thinking. There they are, writing furiously, and not really engaged with the seminar speakers. Their loss, I guess.

You don't need tons of notes. However, you do need to do a brain download of the major themes and takeaways, how they apply to your business, new ideas for articles or products they inspire, what you were thinking, and your intuition during or after the conference. This is where you get the real magic.

If you have attended all-day presentations or a conference, take 15 minutes to capture key notes and feelings and then apply them to your own situation (even if you have a recording or a copy of the presentation). Write notes to yourself and keep them in a file. Share them with your team so everyone can benefit. And best, execute on them immediately.

I keep a conference and course folder to record the good stuff I learn from conferences. But if I haven't moved the information to action (i.e., moved it into something I am working on, or writing about, or getting feedback on) in a short period, then the information does not hold its value for long.

Why stop at just conferences and presentations? You can expand this practice to books and articles you read, courses you take, other great content you find, and ideas you have. Don't just consume information. Get it working for you through smart capturing systems.

While I will admit that my files are not as sophisticated as his, author and educator Tiago Forte has coined a process (and online course and book) he calls "Building a Second Brain." This process uses a structured note-taking system (he encourages the use of note-taking apps) in which you capture materials based on the topics you are focused on and then add notes and build your own personal databank over time, including intermediate "packets" of work (i.e., documentation, articles, presentations) to test ideas, get feedback, repurpose core content, and create momentum for great work.

Machine and Data Capture: From Scanning to Next Gen

If you were to google "documentation capture," you would find many results for software that focuses on scanning technologies. In Information

Management circles, the capturing process has traditionally relied upon scanning technologies (yawn) or importing documents into a content system.

The definition of machine capture is broadening and blurring as our world becomes more data-centric. This is a vast area where companies like Amazon, Facebook, and Google are showing just how much power data delivers.

Machine capture—or other terms like data analytics, data science, Big Data, and artificial intelligence (AI)—are business-world game changers. This book is not dedicated to data capture and analytics. However, this is a huge area that intersects with the documentation space. Machine capture is a large and growing area of documentation in the Information Management circle of the Documentation Triad.

Remember this: there is currently no technology that can really capture information directly from the human brain (although I'm sure Elon Musk is working on this). Machines can capture data, but only humans can capture information. At least, so far.

And that leads us to effective methods for capturing information with note-taking.

4 GUIDELINES FOR SMARTER, FASTER, AND BETTER NOTE-TAKING

Back in the day, while most teens were into Guns N' Roses or Pearl Jam, I had a nerdy fascination with taking notes. This interest grew in high school and university, where it occurred to me that my note-taking prowess gave me a distinct edge over the others in my class. That skill serves me well to this very day. I still stop and ask myself who in this meeting room, presentation, conference, seminar, or Zoom or Teams call is paying attention, and what are we each going to do with this information?

This may come as a shock to you, especially if you are an upper-echelon organization member who doesn't take a lot of notes and you *haven't* taken it seriously until now. Note-taking is a highly underrated skill, especially in today's knowledge-based economy. Your note-taking skills are vital for being smarter in meetings, interviews, courses, conferences, sales calls, and a host of other business scenarios. The notes you take become building blocks for creating documents and for solving your problem at hand. The better you take notes, the better you solve your problems.

If you still don't think note-taking is a big deal, think about the role of Corporate Secretary in your organization. This is the most senior legal position, and the person who oversees a corporation's minutes, policies, and relationship with its Board of Directors. Their main job? To take notes. (While you are at it, explore the definition of "secretary" even further. The Secretary of State and the Secretary of Labor are some of the most powerful positions in the US government. And guess what they control? Government records— aka documentation.)

A comment about "meeting notes" versus "minutes": You will notice I don't use the term "minutes" in this book, and that is intentional. There is a time and a place for minutes-style notes (i.e., board meetings), but they are not useful for most meetings that require a dynamic approach.

Whatever your role, there are two note-taking styles you need to learn and two sets of tools you need to know.

Spotlight Style (Hone Your High-Powered Filter)

I call the first and recommended style of meeting notes the "Spotlight" style. This is when you go into a meeting with a specific purpose or clear outcomes, and you write down key information only. This is what you probably do anyways. As you know, 20 percent at most (and that is generous) of the information from your meetings is relevant to you.

In today's age of distraction, your ability to listen will make you more valuable in your career. Shining your "spotlight" requires intense listening that goes beyond "active listening." If you are an engineer, you are listening for design flaws. If you are an auditor, you are listening for issues. If you are in sales, you are listening to what your customer needs and what you can sell them.

Using the Spotlight style means developing your very own high-powered filter. There's no magic formula for doing this. Through practice and effort, you learn to filter what information you want to bring into your project, your role, and your life. And you filter what you want to leave behind.

When to use the Spotlight style:
- In meetings you are running
- In meetings with a clear purpose or questions to discuss
- During presentations or seminars
- At team meetings, when you are capturing specific action items

Floodlight Style (Write as You Hear It)

The second note-taking style I call the "Floodlight" style. It is about writing what is being said, as it is said. Think of literally flooding your notes onto your page.

If you go to a lot of meetings, this won't be your default approach (or you will frazzle yourself). You probably don't use Floodlight if you are an executive or business leader because you have honed your professional filter over time. But this method works wonders if you are new in a career or (even if you *are* experienced) new in your role, industry, project, or organization.

It doesn't matter how senior you are, sometimes you walk into meetings and need to drink from the fire hose, as they say. You don't know what the problem is, or where the meeting is going, or what the heck people are talking about—and you need to do something or start somewhere. This is about "doing what you can." And then write, write, write.

The Floodlight style is a great teacher of how people process information as a group. People talk in circles, and this can be unproductive, yes. But it is how we humans circuitously coalesce upon an idea or direction.

When to use the Floodlight style:
- In projects or teams that are new to you
- In meetings where the subject is new or difficult and you are learning
- During meetings without a clear purpose
- At meetings when you are asked to "scribe" the notes
- At meetings where you are trying to stay awake (I know this sounds terrible, but it's true)

Pen-and-Paper Approach (Pull Out Your Notebook)

You may be a millennial or Gen Zer reading this and wondering why I am even mentioning pen and paper. Maybe you don't even own pens or paper. Well, hear me out. The pen is not dead. Neither is paper. There are advantages of pen and paper that your MacBook Pro can't beat.

Facebook COO Sheryl Sandberg brings a spiral notebook to her meetings. There are many reasons notebooks work, even for high-tech leaders. Note-taking by hand forces us to think about what we are writing down. This is backed by research. Many studies have concluded that students who took notes by hand remember what they learned in class way better than students who took notes by computer. This is no different at the office. Our pens and paper force the hamsters in our brains to process information more deliberately and with more solid mental links.

I was recently working with a group of intelligent, young, and expensive consultants. They were avid computer-in-meetings users. I sat in meetings like a dinosaur with my old-school notebook and pen. At the end of a few weeks, while the young, expensive consultants had a lot of notes and pretty presentations, they were unable to diagnose issues and design the processes that the client needed. But I was. For effectiveness—and even efficiency—in the long run, you need to use the method that gives you the depth of understanding you need to be successful.

Now, the bad side of pen and paper. You need to manage those notes. I take a lot of hand-written notes, and they are typically all over my desk. But fear not. You will learn how to apply the 24-Hour Rule just ahead.

When to Use the Pen-and-Paper Approach:

- In meetings you are running
- During meetings when establishing chemistry and connection are important
- At meetings or interviews when you are thinking through a technical subject

Technology-Driven Approach (Type It Up)

Your laptop (or other device) is often your most expedient option and makes your desk look a heck of a lot neater than mine. If you are an efficiency junkie or a neat freak, or if your meetings are more about status updates, you might be a new-school laptop-type meeting person. Using a laptop or other technology focuses on the final product and gets you to send out your notes, update your memo, and correct your report faster.

Now, there's a bigger downside to your laptop beyond just impairing your brain hamsters. Your laptop can hurt your connection with your audience. Bringing a laptop to a meeting can make you look more interested in your efficiency (and your screen) than in your team. Some of us in the older generation find typing in a meeting to be rude. And of course (as you know), any tool is just another risk of distraction. That two-second "glance" at an email, a chat message, or NBA highlights might cost you the pearl of information you came to the meeting for.

When to Use a Technology-Driven Approach:
- In meetings you aren't running
- During meetings with nontechnical discussions, like status meetings
- At all-day sessions where you are asked to record a lot of notes
- At meetings when you are asked to "scribe" what is said

Choosing the Right Note-Taking Style and Tool

So, what is the best note-taking style and tool for you? Are you a minimalist or a detail junkie? Are you a traditionalist or trendsetter?

Whatever way you work, experiment with the four guidelines—Spotlight, Floodlight, Pen and Paper, and Technology-Driven—to find your sweet spot.

Most of us will prefer one style or tool over the other, or even blend the styles and methods over time. I personally use a mix of all four options, depending on the meeting. I encourage you and your team members to experiment with what works best.

In March 2020, the world saw a dramatic shift in its meeting and work practices with the onset of the COVID-19 pandemic. The pandemic challenged our meeting practices to the core, and I too felt the need to shift and challenge my approaches. The best method for meeting notes, even in the remote world, remains Spotlight. But you have a bit more opportunity to pull out Floodlight when people can't see you write or type (often when your camera is off).

Snapshot of Dynamic Note-Taking Styles and Tools

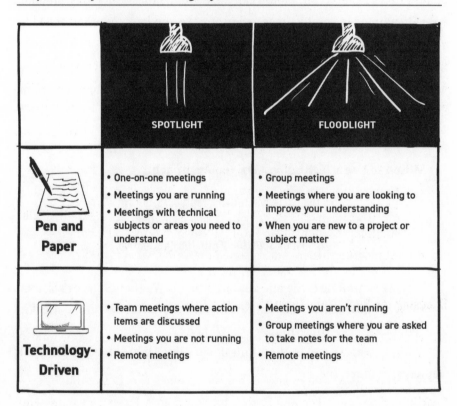

	SPOTLIGHT	FLOODLIGHT
Pen and Paper	• One-on-one meetings • Meetings you are running • Meetings with technical subjects or areas you need to understand	• Group meetings • Meetings where you are looking to improve your understanding • When you are new to a project or subject matter
Technology-Driven	• Team meetings where action items are discussed • Meetings you are not running • Remote meetings	• Meetings you aren't running • Group meetings where you are asked to take notes for the team • Remote meetings

Because comprehension is more important than straight-up time efficiency for most of the problem-solving work I do, I tend to lean more on analog methods. Plus, my computer is a huge distraction for me, and I hate lugging it into meetings. But I will admit that in the remote world, with access to double monitors and the mute button (I am a particularly loud typist), these new challenges have made me more of a new-school person.

The dynamic note-taking method allows you to put more faith in driving action from your notes than in the notes themselves. The notes are just a conduit or segue to the action you need to take. You will refine your note-taking techniques and learn how to work magic with them in the next chapter, Structuring.

For now, understand that you need to have something to work with to start this magic. Need a summary of what to do? Use the snapshot table on page 71.

THE 24-HOUR RULE

By themselves, great notes don't make for better results and smarter organizations. Those great notes need to move you into *action*. That's where the all-important 24-Hour Rule comes into play.

We learned the rule in chapter 1, but let's take a look at it again.

━━━➤ The 24-Hour Rule ◄━━━

states that you *must* rethink, reprocess, or rewrite
information within 24 hours of hearing it. (Or in simpler
terms: just do *something* with the information.)

The 24-Hour Rule is the nucleus of capturing. Without it, your ability to capture the information that matters in your day is like chasing butterflies (i.e., your chances are fleeting).

Now, let's break the 24-Hour Rule down. Here's what I mean by rethink, reprocess, and rewrite.

Rethink

Rethinking means taking a strategic pause every day to reflect on the last 24 hours. What meetings did you go to? Who did you talk to? What did you read, listen to, or learn? What ideas, learnings, intuition, and actions did you encounter? What does this mean to your team, project, or plans?

Build rethinking into your daily routine. It may mean spending a few minutes at the beginning or end of each day to think about what was said (and not said), decided (or not decided), or understood (or not understood). Start small. A minute or two per meeting is enough to get you on your way.

Rethinking often drives reprocessing or rewriting. If it drives neither, ask yourself whether your meetings, courses, or conversations could have been more productive, insightful, or action-oriented.

The habit is more critical nowadays in the WFH world, where we have less of the water cooler chat to reminisce about "How did you think that meeting went?"

Rethinking within a 24-hour window gives you a new and fresh perspective—one removed from the biased perspective that arises in the heat of the meeting, conversation, or presentation.

Reprocess

Reprocessing is about moving your notes to the right place. If you scribbled them on a piece of paper, you may want to type them up. If you took them on a computer, you could copy them to a document you are working on. If you heard action items, move them to your to-do list or project plan.

Maybe you don't need any notes at all. In this case, just tackle the action items—the quick email, the report to send, the easy administrative task—within 24 hours to eliminate backlog before it piles up.

Don't wait. Put the 24-Hour Rule into action as soon as possible and get it working *for* you right away.

Rewrite

Rewriting is about stepping back and saying what you heard in your own voice and through your own lens. This is where the magic happens.

Your rewritten notes will look very different from the actual sequence of the conversation of your meeting. They will be a summary, a paraphrase, or a few bullet notes of what you heard.

Use the opportunity to interject your own thoughts and concepts into what was said. For example, a client wants to "tighten procedures" next month. What does that mean? How does that impact you and your team? Expand and interpret what you heard or understood. This is an analysis, not a rote exercise.

WHY THE 24-HOUR RULE?

After 24 hours (or less!), our short-term memory starts declining. The longer you wait past 24 hours to document your notes, update your analysis, track your to-dos, or file that form, the harder it gets. But there are more reasons beyond just the limitations of short-term memory.

We Turbocharge Our Momentum

Have you ever had something that sat on your to-do list for weeks that you just couldn't seem to get to? But then, a new task—ah, adrenaline burst—comes your way and you attack it with record speed?

We have an energetic connection with information—tasks, projects, ideas—that we hear in a 24-hour window. However, the longer you wait past 24 hours, the harder it gets.

There will be times when you will have to fight with every inch of your body to move a task forward.

So, take advantage of the momentum of recency while you've got it. Surf that wave. Ride with the wind at your back. Excuse the metaphors. But the point is to recognize momentum as fleeting and precious. Don't squander it.

Where can you do a better job of working in the 24-Hour Rule?

- **Sales.** You go to a sales meeting. Write back to the prospect in 24 hours. Or log the prospects or potential projects in your sales system in 24 hours.

- **Business analyst.** After an interview, document your notes in 24 hours so you don't forget the nuances. If you can, write back to your interviewees in 24 hours.
- **Business owner and checking in on employees.** Email or review the work or progress of your employees within 24 hours.
- **Administrative and paperwork.** Paper comes into your office, like a request for a quote. Your team can adopt a process of dealing with (i.e., filing, entering, processing) the paperwork (e.g., sales orders, invoices, receipts) within 24 hours.
- **Email.** A 24-hour turnaround on your emails is, for many of us, a reasonable turnaround time. It typically keeps your boss, clients, and coworkers happy but still allows you plenty of time in the day for thinking and focus.

It's a Gauge on Reality

Imagine a factory. It has a conveyor belt on which widget parts are coming into the factory every day. But the outgoing conveyor belt is broken. More and more widgets pile up daily, creating a jam in the whole system.

Does this remind you of your work?

For most of us, the jam will never be fully detected. But it will drain your energy, productivity, and success over the long run.

Simple math will tell you that if you keep piling on to-dos in your day, but you aren't moving enough out in 24 hours, this system isn't going to work.

Use the 24-Hour Rule as a reality check on your schedule and a gauge on your to-dos.

If your schedule is so packed with meetings that you can't even take 1 minute (let's start small) to think about each meeting you had, then *Houston, we have a problem!* Your conveyor belt will clog soon.

I originally wrote the 24-Hour Rule specifically for meeting or interview notes. But there is wider and deeper application to our human workflow. A friend of mine has a creative use for the 24-Hour Rule to get control of her to-do list. She only takes on tasks she can get done within 24 hours to eliminate a pile of half-done projects.

It's a Superpower, Even If It's Not Perfect

If you can embrace the 24-Hour Rule, you will move into the ranks of super-producer and elite performer. You don't need to be last year's salesperson of the year. Or the most technical on your team. Or the most educated.

The 24-Hour Rule is a Little d practice that makes your team better, too. How your team acts in 24-hour increments is what will determine its success or failure. Not your metadata or file structure or elaborate system. You can implement the greatest incident management system, but if no one logs issues that come up, it won't be worth anything. You can implement the fanciest document repository, but if your team doesn't contribute to it daily, you have wasted your time.

Your 24-Hour Rule muscle and that of your team will develop with time and practice. It took me time to get faster at processing my notes and conversations, but after 16 years of practice, I have developed a habit of processing what has come into my day in the past 24 hours. And I am the Energizer Bunny on my keyboard.

The 24-hour processor is not a perfect system. You will fall down. Your team will mess up. You won't feel like reviewing your meetings or reprocessing what was said yesterday on many (if not most) days. It will be hard—even impossible—to process everything in 24 hours on many days, too. But it is better than having no system at all. It is better than just letting your notes, ideas, to-dos, documents, projects, meetings, and family work just keep piling up and up with no chance of resolution or resurrection.

The 24-Hour Rule isn't a modern, tech-savvy, or silver-bullet rule. But the 24-Hour Rule isn't inefficient, either. What is truly inefficient is bouncing from meeting to meeting, call to call, conference to conference, course to course, seminar to seminar, conversation to conversation without doing anything with the information.

Now *that* is a tragic waste. Not only of your time at work, but also of your life.

WHAT *NOT* TO CAPTURE

Deciding what *not* to put on paper is important.

Can you imagine a recorder for all thoughts, meetings, and what you ate or drank or interactions with your spouse, kids, and people in your home? You would be overwhelmed. Discernment means good judgment on what to capture. Editorial judgment, if you will.

I love putting things into writing. But (there is always a "but," isn't there?) putting things into writing has power. There are legal, reputational, relational, and ethical factors involved here, too. Don't capture everything, since certain business documents, such as emails, are discoverable. Are you hitting the "record" button for every Zoom meeting?

Let's discuss.

Off-the-Record Conversations

So, you heard confidential or personal information in a meeting that you technically weren't supposed to hear? Don't write it down. Off-the-record comments are off the record for a reason. They are not always a bad thing. Gossip (if not mean-spirited) has value. Whoever told you the information had a reason for doing so, typically involving giving you insight on the topic at hand. There may be a valid business reason they are sharing something with you.

I have read that some experts recommend bringing machine recorders to meetings, which will spit out the full conversation. I disagree with this approach for almost all meetings, because people will hold back on what they say out of caution when they know they are on record (although it works for some limited contexts, like when you're bringing in an expert). Not only will you miss out on juicy gossip, but you will also waste your team's time by having to relisten to the meeting when you likely will have only two or three notes.

Legal Implications

Documentation can help you defend yourself or your company in the case of arbitration, litigation, or a malpractice lawsuit. It can also keep you out of court in the first place.

But documentation can hang you from a legal perspective, too. If you are dealing with sensitive discussions, such as which contractors to pay or not, there are times when you should definitely not record these conversations or put them in writing. You should always discuss with your legal department the best course of action.

While it goes against my primal instincts, which encourage companies to commit more to writing, I have had to write processes for clients that instruct team members to use verbal communications around certain financial, human resources, or "privileged" (i.e. necessitating lawyer involvement in orchestrating the process) discussions where there is a risk of running afoul of legalities, or in matters of arbitration or litigation.

There are also various laws that protect an individual's privacy by setting out rules for collection, fair use, or disclosure of personal information by public bodies. So, be very careful not to capture information that could put you on the wrong side of these laws.

Bad News, Arguments, and Personal Vendettas

Would you document the worst argument you had with your spouse? When it comes to bad news or arguments, please don't email or text, just pick up the phone or talk it out in person.

If you are reprimanding a coworker or disagreeing with them, meet with them in person or pick up the phone. In these cases, avoid documentation where you can, unless it is required for performance reporting or human resources. Documentation is very, very powerful, because it can't be taken back. A conversation can be forgotten, but documentation can live forever. You think you're safe because you deleted that questionable email? Think again. And remember that emails are discoverable.

Widely Available—or Marginal—Information

Do you really need to waste your precious Paris vacation taking pictures of the Eiffel Tower? You can find thousands of pictures online (probably much better than the blurry one you just took). If it lives on the web, you don't need to write it down, either.

There is one exception to this statement. As we talked about under the Floodlight note-taking approach, sometimes we write to reinforce the concepts in our own minds. This might be a technique you used in school to understand calculus, physics, or social sciences. Using this approach, we aren't planning on "using" our notes; we are putting the note-taking process to work to hammer down the concepts.

Using documentation as a hammer is OK, but if the information already exists somewhere, like in the presentation, in an existing process, or on the web, you probably don't need to write it down. Likewise, don't become a documentation dork, documenting for documentation's sake. Don't set yourself up for failure. Document what truly matters. Otherwise, you're not helping yourself or others, and you're not being smart.

Capturing is the key to successful Dynamic Documentation. It is a Little d practice that you and your team members need to learn in order to have Big D results down the road. Intelligent use of brain dumps, interviews, note-taking, and faithfulness to the 24-Hour Rule will net you immediate gains in clarity, efficacy, and results. Then you can start to "clean up" the content messes and ideas you've captured to make even bigger headway.

And that is where structure comes into play.

CHAPTER 4

Structuring

Build fast, fill in, rinse, repeat.

F orm follows function. All the greatest breakthroughs in the world—in science, business, entrepreneurship, technology, and the arts—have come from structuring unstructured information into something beautiful and, ultimately, useful, finding patterns where none had been seen before. You too can create great things from seeing creative patterns in information using Dynamic Documentation.

Now that you have your documentation captured, the "Structure" step is about shuffling, moving, pulling together, and looking for patterns and "magic" in the information you've got in front of you.

Gaps in structuring may show up as:

- Weak analysis of problems
- Inability to create documents from scratch
- Inability to design processes or systems
- Inability to get started on documents, systems, or projects
- Poorly constructed documents
- Using the wrong types of documents

Like capturing, weaknesses in structuring will likely go undetected in your organization. No one will realize that it's a lack of structuring skills that is leading to bloated (or Stage 5 "Overkill") or circling Big D system implementations, documentation programs, or audits. You need the Little d skills of iterating, building, and pattern recognition to get on track.

These days, we are bombarded with information, surrounded as we are by devices and platforms. It's like we're stuck in a video game, fighting information gunfire and dodging distraction booby traps. The good news is that our brains have the ability to filter and structure this information even when it is firing at us. Having this ability and actually doing something about it are two different things, however.

Although it may seem counterintuitive, if you are in a job where you have routine tasks or clearly defined orders, you may not have developed a strong ability to structure information. Unstructured environments are another story. They can be the best teachers to build our "structure chops." Writing reports, creating products, developing new websites, or even starting new businesses are some of the best examples.

The words "Scotland Yard" may evoke images of London wreathed in fog, killers stalking, and cobbled streets. The early Scotland Yard is the home of one of the world's first organized detective forces. Its famous detectives inspired works like the Sherlock Holmes stories as well as many other London-based crime novels. Mystery aside, these detectives were some of the early adopters of Dynamic Documentation techniques. For one, they were the first police force to have organized record keeping (i.e., capturing). With this record keeping, they were able to take bits of information, piece them together, and solve crimes (i.e., through structuring).

You may not be solving murders when you go to work (unless you are a detective reading this book). But it doesn't hurt to see the information in your organization like a mystery full of "clues" you need to piece together—be it understanding why there is a dip in sales, why a process is inefficient, or why employees are not adopting the new system.

A STEP-BY-STEP FORMULA FOR CREATING A DYNAMIC DOCUMENT

Although a well-structured document should end up looking like a series of clearly connected thoughts and ideas leading to a natural, logical conclusion, this is not how it starts out. The author of the document starts with a pile of puzzle pieces that need to be strategically put together. Often, there is no map to guide construction of the end product.

Once you capture your initial information, structuring helps you to see where you are, gives you a framework for elaboration, and sets in motion the

7 Steps to Creating a Dynamic Document

1 State the purpose

2 Identify the appropriate template

3 Slap down captured information

4 Flesh out

6 Flag gap areas

Enhance and fill in **5**

7 Rigorously review

process of getting input from others. Of course, this means writing, which follows the notes you've captured.

Being a good "writer" is more about being a good "structurer" than anything else. Making words sound nice is the easy part; structuring is the "meat" of writing. Structuring lets you take seemingly meaningless content and turn it into useful documents.

It's difficult to create a document from scratch. Many successful professionals don't know where to start. Writer's block is a real issue, not merely the stuff of Hollywood screenplay legend.

If this sounds even remotely familiar, take heart: what follows is the 7-step formula for creating a dynamic document.

Step 1. State the Purpose

Why are you working on this document in the first place? If you are assigning the task of creating this document to a team member, you need to be clear on that purpose, too. Go back to the problem you are trying to solve. A document should serve the following purposes:

- Changing or influencing behaviors (e.g., policy, process, procedure)
- Organizing tasks or steps (e.g., project plan, task list, requirements)
- Conceptualizing information or ideas (e.g., memo, analysis)
- Providing useful instructions (e.g., a reference guide)
- Communicating key messages (e.g., corporate communications)

Many times, especially earlier in my career, I have experienced the feeling of not really understanding why we were working on certain documents. To name a few examples, I have been asked to:

- Create communications no one will ever read
- Build fancy presentations that have no substance
- Update status reports when there is nothing to update
- Complete lengthy matrixes that did not support the analysis we were working on

Sound familiar? Documents that lack a "why" may reveal deep-seated project issues and misunderstandings between you and your manager or team leader as well. Speak up! Earlier in my career, I would go along with creating anything my boss or client asked for. I started to notice that the documents I didn't see the point to (rightfully or not) were harder for me to do well. I'd lose interest and have trouble getting them done.

If you see this pattern in your own work, you might have a problem in the design of your project from the get-go, or you may need to better explain the value of the project to your team. Starting with the "why" is critical for driving your structure—it will be at the back of your team's minds and will lead them more easily to a better document. If the purpose of your document is to train, then let's start there.

Step 2. Identify the Appropriate Template

Now that you know why you are working on the document, you can identify and implement the perfect template (a deep dive into this follows). For certain documents like an analysis, a memo, or a story, you might not have a "template" but rather an "outline." An outline can be a rough sketch of what you want to say. A couple points or scribbles to manage your structure is all you need to get started.

Step 3. Slap Down Captured Information

Now is the time to pull out that great information you trapped during the Capture phase. "Slap down" your information into the document or system. Move quickly. This may be information from your interview notes, meeting notes, emails, other research, or a combination of a few sources. In some cases, this information might only be stored in your mental hard drive.

Slapping down is a powerful way of building momentum. I was once working with a team building a new pipeline (kind of like a company inside a bigger company). Even though they were working inside a big company, they were essentially a Stage 1 team, as they were building their documents from scratch. When I arrived on the team, they had a few false starts with their process design because the team was focused on how different and complex this new entity was. The team had a mantra that they were "building the plane as they were flying it." This was true in many respects. But the "airplane parts" were in fact not new. I took the opposite approach to drive the processes forward. I started with what we knew (not with what we didn't) to pull together templates, information, existing concepts, or similar procedures. This soon gave us a clear line of sight into what we knew and what we needed to figure out. This put us many flying miles ahead of where we were a few weeks earlier.

Step 4. Flesh Out

You should now be looking at a document that has notes slapped down into it. The grammar and the sentence structure won't be perfect on the first go-around. Write out sentences to make your document read better and faster. As you grow in your capacity to turn around great notes, you will find over time that your notes are more and more relevant and useful for building out your document.

Step 5. Enhance and Fill In

Think of this as "stretching" the content. Enhancing and "filling in" is where you use educated guesses and your professional judgment to expand on the information you have.

As an accountant, I have looked at hundreds of accounts payable processes. If I collect some points on how the process works, I can probably fill in the blanks. Do the same depending on your expertise to fill in the plan, change analysis, process, policy, design document, or whatever else you are working on. If your educated guesses need to be adjusted, there will be lots of opportunities for people to polish the final product.

━━━ Use What You Know Draft ━━━

This means that you build your first drafts of documents
based on what you know, using the information you
have and your experiences and instincts.

Don't wait until you are 100 percent sure about something to write it down. 100 percent certainty is an impossible goal. As is often said, "Don't let perfect be the enemy of good."

I was working for a large company on a process that was reasonably technical and new and involved different parties. I sat in my boss's office, and we mocked up the process on her whiteboard in about an hour. I used educated guesses to draft an initial document and sent it back to her, and in two days, we had a solid draft for circulation by Friday of that week.

I received a call on Monday that another team was working on the same new process. They had planned to spend *six months* on it! This group used a totally different technique. The business analyst held large sessions. He interviewed everyone. He discussed every detail before writing anything down. The result was that it took nearly thirty times as long to produce their document. That is the difference between a lean, dynamic approach that leverages stretching and smart guesswork and an approach that goes for the detail. Truth be told, we both got to exactly the same place. But it took my team a fraction of the time. Be the judge of what technique works for you. Using educated stretches saves you significant time.

Step 6. Flag Gap Areas

Gap areas are different from enhancement areas because you can't quite make an educated guess as to what is or should be going on in gaps. Gap areas may be things that don't make sense even now that you have put the pieces together (this is a benefit of the Structuring phase). Or they may be things you realize you forgot to ask in your interview. Sometimes, they refer to areas of the document where there is inconsistency, lack of clarity, or contradictory bits of information.

Even if you are a seasoned interviewer, you are likely to have forgotten to ask something you should have in the interview stage. As you are piecing together information from a few different sources, you will also uncover inconsistencies. Relax. This is part of the benefit and magic of writing a document and the structuring process overall.

The process of doing a quick first draft will allow you to find the gaps quickly and address them faster. When you share your document for review, flag your gap areas with a different color (or other marker) than your stretch areas. You may even want to list your gap area questions separately in an email or cover memo. The gap areas will be areas where you have bigger questions and will probably need more discussion.

Step 7. Rigorously Review

Now you can circulate the document back to your stakeholders. Work collaboratively on problem areas you have identified and gather feedback. The idea is to start with a hard push, step back to review, fill in and rework, then iterate and improve. It may take a few rounds depending on the nature of the document.

There you go, you have created a document! These steps will make you a master of the Structuring step of Dynamic Documentation. (In the next step of Dynamic Documentation, "Presenting," you'll learn how to further refine and polish your final product.) You can apply this technique to many areas of your work, all the way from the Little d skills like note-taking or writing an email to the Big D results of processes, procedures, policies, analyses, presentations, and communications.

LEAN DOCUMENTATION

Lean documentation is an approach to building (that is, structuring) your document or document system. It combines Little d individual thinking with how you work with your team (Medium D, perhaps) to how you design Big D implementations, systems, and projects.

Lean documentation is based on the concepts of *The Lean Startup* by Eric Ries, published in 2011. The message is still cutting edge today. *The Lean Startup* challenges the traditional model for product launches (i.e., a long cycle of market research, product development, advertising, and promotion) with a get-it-to-market approach that emphasizes working out the kinks as you go.

I love building great documentation and systems with meaningful content, slick design, and killer visuals. But documentation isn't about perfection. You can't guess perfectly what your people want or how they will use your documents or systems, no matter how long you spend interviewing, workshopping, drawing up requirements, or talking to vendors.

Try spotting "fat projects" in the work world—they usually aren't hard to see, especially if you are working in a Stage 5 (Overkill) environment. I have seen many "fat" documentation projects in my travels. To name a few:

- I have seen documents go through twenty rounds of edits, and then no one reads them anyway.
- I have seen companies spend fortunes on Information Management strategies but never implement them.
- I have seen policies drafted, circulated, and talked about for *years* before getting published. Most of the time, these policies would take only a few days, or even hours, of my actual writing time.
- I have worked with documentation systems that take more time to manage than to create the documents themselves.
- I had a client that would routinely bring about fifteen people together (including a lot of expensive consultants) to review trivial details on their diagrams which were pretty much common sense in the first place. (Have you heard the expression "too many cooks spoil the broth"?)
- I was working as a business analyst in IT service management when my client brought in an expensive senior consultant with beautiful diagramming skills. The problem was that they were diagramming

the most basic concepts (like checking a license) and giving them the complexity of a nuclear reactor project.

- I once had a client who spent five years developing detailed systems mapping with a full project team. The team was holding out for a "complete" project launch and never shared their information. New management took over the IT department and the product never launched. Years of intellectual capital and millions of dollars were burned.

What's the solution? Cut the fat. Get lean.

Let's compare the traditional approach to documentation projects with the lean Dynamic Documentation approach.

Traditional Documentation Projects

This was the approach that I was taught in business school and in business analyst training some years ago. To be clear, this is *not* the approach I recommend.

- **Requirements gathering and business analysis:** Let's agonize over the perfect details of our documentation or system. Hire a business analyst to do months of requirements gathering through fancy workshops.
- **Buy a fancy documentation system:** Let's build a solution to solve everyone's problems. Go through an extensive request-for-proposal (RFP) process. Choose the perfect, top-of-the-line, large-scale system and then spend more money customizing it to meet the company's unique asks.
- **Build perfect documentation:** Let's stress ourselves to death over the perfect details of our documentation—perfect format, perfect system, perfect metadata, perfect content. Solicit feedback from a ton of stakeholders to make everyone feel included. Finalize the product after all details are in a "perfect" state.

- **Launch user-acceptance testing:** Launch the systems or documents and conduct tons of training about how to use them. Hire fancy change management experts to talk to users.
- **Feedback and disbanding:** Send out a few surveys to ask for advice. Disband the project. Hope that the stakeholders use the product or documentation. Cross our fingers.

Lean (or Dynamic) Documentation Projects

Lean documentation is about getting your "product" (your documents and your documentation system) to "market" (typically, your employees in an organization). Then get feedback (many times) to make your product better over time.

- **Design the project and the solutions to be scalable:** Make your solution scalable. Plan the project in chunks, not as a one-shot deal. Don't go for the fanciest system that some vendor is jamming down your throat. Get real on which bells and whistles you really need. Plan implementations where you can get the system to work and then make tweaks as you go.
- **Get your documentation, system, or project to "good enough" for feedback:** Through the scheduled increments of the project, think of getting your documents to "good enough" for use by stakeholders. Don't wait until the final "launch" to share time-sensitive information with the people who need it.
- **Get it out to a real audience for real feedback:** Get the documents or system to your audience for feedback. Then make improvements.
- **Use a feedback loop and tweak:** Revisit your documentation again in a realistic time frame. Build in an annual review cycle for your documentation or document system.

In school, we are marked on a predefined set of work with a hard deadline. This is baloney in the work world, where in most jobs we don't have a limited, defined set of work. In the work world, quality is still important. But the momentum you bring to your organization—often through the structuring process—is more important than the quality of each specific task.

Getting something done that generates momentum for bigger things is more important than crafting the ideal product. Perfection kills the documentation process. I have hired people who have created elaborate walkthrough, process, or testing documentation that cost me days of budget when simple interview notes would have gotten us closer to what we needed.

Getting a lot done is better than getting little done perfectly. The more your team is producing, the more your team is learning and growing, and the quality of their work will improve.

Documentation projects require an entrepreneurial mindset that allows the creator to test them. This mindset thrives in a culture where it is OK to take risks and make mistakes, and where honest, constructive feedback is encouraged. Projects should be iterative. You'll soon see what is working and what isn't. Improve the product as you go.

LEANING INTO (WELL-CHOSEN) TEMPLATES

Templates create or serve a pattern. Technically, a template can help us capture (e.g., structured interviews) and present (e.g., visual layout) information. But I believe the topic belongs under Structuring because templates are such a valuable tool in the process of organizing content and findings.

Here are just a few processes where a template may come in handy, since there are great similarities across industries, and in companies of various sizes.

- **Finance:** Accounts payable, accounts receivable, cash management, budgeting, monthly close, financial statement preparation, authorization for expenditure, purchasing
- **IT:** Change management, system development, problem & incident management, access management

- **HR:** New hire, onboarding, voluntary termination, involuntary termination, annual appraisals, extended sick leave
- **Sales:** Request for proposal, new client onboarding, monthly sales meetings, leads monitoring/generation

Quick note: I am not really talking about "forms" here. Social security numbers, tax returns, and HR paperwork all relate to "forms." While they are part of Information Management, they are not part of Dynamic Documentation.

While not all templates are created equal, templates are a good source of ideas, and that is the priority. They are created by others who have approached a problem or initiative that is like what you are working on. Templates are a device to get you started on a project, approach a problem, design a new process, and interview people.

Well-designed templates help you to visualize large amounts of information and give structure to loose or scattered information. They free you to do great work.

One common example is a project plan that lets you visualize the project activities, people on the team, or the timeline. It allows you to grasp on one page all elements of a project. Another example is a control matrix, which pulls together information on Internal Controls, the design assessment, testing results, and conclusions. One of my clients rolled out intricate new Internal Control software with bells and whistles to replace their control matrixes. Unfortunately, the fancy system took about five times longer to click through the tabs and review information as the simple Excel control matrix did. A simple template often beats complex software.

Templates give you consistency, repeatability, and scale. Professional bodies such as accounting firms, law firms, engineering firms, and larger consulting organizations invest considerably in building templates because they are a source of scale. Using templates allows these firms to pump out mini armies of resources for high fees. You may not be building armies in your current work, but you may have developed documents you can "rinse and repeat" with future projects.

But there is always an "on the other hand" moment, isn't there? And the world of templates is no exception.

A one-size-fits-all approach to templates can be fraught. I once tried to use an IT assessment questionnaire that was comprehensive but focused on all the wrong directions for what the client needed. This proved to be disastrous. By picking the wrong template, I sent the consultant working for me off in the wrong direction.

Overreliance on templates can also be fraught. News flash: The template alone will not do the work. Filling in a pretty template is not going to make people want to adopt a new system or change their behaviors. Realize the limitations of your templates from the start. Templates are not great at communicating, connecting, or enforcing on their own. That takes the finesse and professional expertise only you can provide.

The kissing cousin of template overreliance is template overkill. This is common if you are a company or team in Stage 5, the overkill category. Actually, it is beyond a simple waste of time. It can be downright draining. Too intricate? Too long? Too expensive? Too rigidly formatted? If your team is struggling "just to get through" the templates, they will have no time to do the real work.

Don't forget what we just learned about lean projects, either. In our Internal Control business, I have inherited testing templates from other, bigger firms that are elaborate and quite frankly *gorgeous*. But documentation isn't cheap. Elaborate templates have a high cost of filling-in and maintaining and an even higher cost of sucking up time and brainpower.

While I can't speak for all professions, the accounting and audit world need a shake-up in their philosophies of using templates and training new staff. Templates should be viewed as a source of ideas and tools to help guide their training, and as a means of flexibility, not a source of "truth." This philosophy will help new CPAs get the best of both worlds of structure and creativity to grow their professional judgment and common sense.

Caveats duly noted, it is time to place templates into perspective, and put them to work.

- **Identify one or more templates to start from:** Assuming you aren't required by corporate edict to use one template, search online or ask professional associates for suggestions on the best template for you. Even if you are assigned a template, there is no harm in looking for comparable options.

- **Adapt and modify for your current need:** Once you've identified potential templates, analyze what they offer versus what you need. Have you ever started a survey but realized you need to answer fifty questions that all seem the same? A shorter survey is typically more successful at getting a good response rate and getting the answers you need.

- **Allow for variation:** A template is not a prison cell (or a set of handcuffs, for that matter). Allow flexibility in using the template. If the template will be used by your staff to conduct interviews, then let them ask questions in congruence with their personalities.

- **Evaluate, build, and update your template library:** Remember, too, that the use of templates is a living process. Periodically evaluate how your templates are working and collect feedback. Build a library of reusable templates for your team. Remember, templates are about scale!

STRUCTURING CONTENT WITHIN DOCUMENTS

Structuring content within documents is about taking information you have and then moving it around to the best format, sequence, template, or outline you can. Here is where you can take your Little d ability to intelligently structure information and move it into the best Big D format for your team, department, or organization.

There are two ways of thinking about structuring content that are equally useful. I use either technique depending on the context and the needs of my audience.

Modular, or "Chunky" Documents

The first way to approach structuring documents is to focus on a popular Information Management concept called "modular" documentation, or as I like to call it, "chunky" documentation. This is about breaking out your information into digestible modules, or "chunks." This works for you if you are designing a library (e.g., for templates, sales materials, or reference materials) or your team is wrestling with cumbersome documents.

I once worked with the sales team of a large IT service provider. The vice president was concerned about the quality of the proposal and marketing information being sent to her customers and the amount of time it was taking her team to look for materials and turn around requests. I collected materials from across the company, curated the best stuff, broke it out, edited it, created a SharePoint site, and added metadata. We used a modular concept where the sales team could pull small chunks of information based on what they were looking at, including location, service line, expertise, and technology.

The sales team loved the site and adopted it immediately. This process strengthened the quality and speed of the materials and the company's success rate overall. (They even had to turn away new business a year later.)

What are the advantages of using modular documentation?

- Reusable and recyclable content (e.g., available off intranets or SharePoint sites)
- Digestible content (i.e., easy to use and apply to other work)
- Helpful reference materials (e.g., for sales, best practices, templates)
- Faster content edits and updates

Larger, Omnibus Documents

While you will find a lot written about modular documentation, you will not find this technique of bigger, omnibus documents taught in any traditional Information Management books or courses. Creating larger, omnibus or one-stop-shop documents is the opposite technique of modular documentation.

You will often not find it practical to hand your boss or client (or many others for that matter) fifty separate documents. A comprehensive document may be what you need to distribute, get consensus on, and speed up decisions or understanding of the content.

I was working with a large oil company in a role that covered IT governance, audit, and the compliance team. While the company had hundreds of IT and accounting documents, my client had the sense that no one really knew how IT worked and how it impacted accounting. (He was right.) I created an "IT application and interface manual" that pulled together key information on IT applications and interfaces, along with high-level diagrams to support how the information flowed. I explained how these applications supported the business and the "so what" of why we are looking at applications (e.g., some handle billions of dollars, some millions, and some thousands, but most of the audit and governance teams didn't know the difference).

This easy-to-read, nontechnical fifty-page manual ended up being a big support for training and clarifying with the auditors, the IT team, accounting, and the SOX and compliance teams. When team members read the document, most claimed that they "knew it all along" (although they didn't). But this is the journey of a documenter, especially when you learn how to structure larger, omnibus documents. You make it look too easy.

What are the advantages of larger, more cohesive documentation?

- One-stop shop for reading about an area, issue, or plan
- Shareable content, specifically for management
- Support for a central theme or decision
- Control over one document (not many)

You've harnessed your creativity to gather your information (Capturing) and shaped it so it is easily accessed and used to best advantage (Structuring). It's time to take your personal Little d skills and your ability to work "leanly" with your team and organization to build great Big D projects, systems, and documents. Now let's grab your reader and "sell" this great information you've accumulated.

It's time to learn how to present.

CHAPTER 5

Presenting

Curb appeal sells.

apturing and structuring are the blueprints, foundation, carpentry, and plumbing of your house. "Presenting" is the paint, landscaping, and interior design. Presenting is what "sells" your valuable information to your team. A proper presentation gives it *curb appeal*, to continue the real estate metaphor.

A house built upon a flawed foundation won't hold. But a house isn't a home without the pizzazz of *presentation*. A document is no different. Technical information alone won't make your reader fall in love with it, much less engage with it. You want your audience to accept your information, share it, and use it regularly.

Presenting is about dynamic writing (how the content is expressed) and dynamic design (aesthetic considerations). Once you've gotten the core content of your document structured and filled in, you will want to polish your product before it's presented to a larger group.

Let's look at the documentation problem you are working on again. What are the possible symptoms of a "Presenting" problem, assuming that the people who need the information know the material exists and understand where it can be found?

Gaps in presenting skills may show up as:

- No one is reading your documents.
- Your documents or document systems are forgettable.
- Your documents take a long time to read (perhaps they are too dense).
- Your message is not jumping out (you're "burying the lede," as my journalist friends might say: hiding the most important points deep in the document).
- People don't recall (or cannot recall) what was said in your documents. Even if they get the message, your work is forgettable.

Organizations spend boatloads on Big D process redesigns, training, procedures, diagrams, and presentations in the name of "getting documented." But then—the tragedy—the documents just sit there collecting digital dust. Don't let this happen to your work. Use the Little d skills of engaging writing, visual flair, and connection with your audience to make your Big D projects pull their weight.

You don't need to be a professional writer and you don't need to spend years in journalism or design school to improve your material. You don't even need to create long documents. There are lots of ways to share information, including lists and email, that can still practice the secrets of writers and designers.

And if you're *still* anxious about your writing or design abilities, remember to take advantage of skill stacking, which we discussed in chapter two. Dynamic Documentation is not a solo sport.

You can build your and your team's skills while combining strengths. Team up with one or more colleagues who are strong in writing, editing, graphics, illustration, or layout to crystallize your materials. And remember, for Dynamic Documentation, the focus is on your message, not on your award-winning literary and graphic design abilities.

Keep your goal in mind. Does the document say what it needs to say in a way that connects with, teaches, and motivates its intended audience? Let's return to the 5 Super Standards. With the exception of the Findability

Standard, all of these apply to presenting. Use these standards to help you rate your work, or ask a trusted colleague to vet your material:

- **Clarity Standard:** Does my audience understand what I am talking about? Can the audience understand the key concepts quickly without having to reread it? Are they "getting it"?
- **Engagement Standard:** Is the document connecting with my reader? Are the key messages and concepts resonating? Does my reader remember the document and its contents?
- **Re-Performance Standard:** Can my reader perform a task based on the document? Do these steps help them with their jobs?
- **Use Standard:** Do people like this document enough to use it?

Let's first look at the content. The words.

DYNAMIC WRITING

Ask yourself: Why does your coworker book a meeting when she could have written a short memo? Why do your consultants flood their presentations with fancy graphics? Because writing is hard and dynamic writing is harder still.

Dynamic writing is a hybrid form that borrows the best from a range of writing disciplines, including technical writing, copywriting, blogging, and even journalism. Technical writing is about writing for technical fields (e.g., accounting, IT, engineering). Copywriting is about writing to sell. Blogging and journalism are about stories, experiences, reporting hard news, and offering opinions.

Dynamic writing is about writing to benefit your audience. It's about clear, compelling communication of complex information. It's about drawing your reader in and holding their attention. It's about writing to a human being, not an organization.

Unfortunately, there is no app you can download to get your dynamic writing style. Developing your own writing style takes Little d practice, persistence, pounding the keys, as well as studying the work of others. You know your audience. You understand what they need to know and what they don't know. Rely on your gut and your professional experience. Develop the cadence, sound, look, humor, and personality that will resonate with your audience.

Be true to yourself. You will stand out as a person among information "parrots" and corporate androids.

Dynamic Writing Code

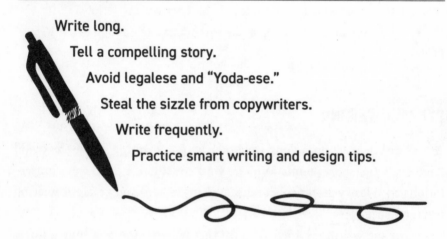

Write long.

Tell a compelling story.

Avoid legalese and "Yoda-ese."

Steal the sizzle from copywriters.

Write frequently.

Practice smart writing and design tips.

Start with Too Much (or "Write Long")

You may be surprised to learn that professional writers are comfortable throwing away large portions of their work. It is called "writing long." The editing process will help you see what sections need trimming, as well as those that need a bit of fleshing out.

Break the procrastination cycle: In the business world, we are too concerned about getting everything down on paper, so we just don't get started. Procrastination constipation. We agonize over each word. Or worse, we have a meeting to discuss putting down the first word.

As with every form of writing, dynamic writing is about rewriting. No one gets it "right" on the first draft. No one. Do not hit "send" until you have reviewed your work. Wait. Then return to your work and edit it with fresh eyes.

Rewriting may be daunting, especially if you're thinking, "I just want to document, not be the next Malcolm Gladwell!" To build a great document— be it a memo, a business case, an article, or even a spreadsheet—you need to start with too much, knowing that the editing process is the next step. You will move things around dramatically. You will replace. You will cut, cut, cut to unearth the gold buried in your work.

Your first draft will not be seen by anyone but you. And you will be the first person to shape this document and make it ready for prime time.

Just *start*.

For Crying Out Loud, Tell a Compelling Story!

Channel the secrets of great bloggers and journalists. Hook your reader and do it fast. Consider this: The attention spans of most readers are shorter than ever. Longform text has become an obstacle rather than a benefit. In this, the Age of the Tweet, well-written documents—especially lengthy ones—are few and far between.

In other words, get to the point, and fast. Hook them and explain, "Here is why you need to know this."

- **Build a pyramid:** Get to the meat of the matter, and then substantiate it. Think of your work as a pyramid of information. The top of the pyramid contains the most important parts—what your audience needs to know first and foremost. Supporting material follows, as the pyramid shape broadens.
- **Reel them in with great titles, subtitles, email subject lines, and headlines:** For a blogger, a killer title means the difference between zero or a million clicks. Adding a compelling title, subtitle, email subject line, or headline is a secret weapon to spark your

dynamic writing. A great title is like the perfect accessory with your favorite black dress or black suit. Want to know their secrets? Use what bloggers call the 4 Us: be Unique, Useful, Ultra-Specific, and Urgent. Practice these additional tips shared by bloggers and journalists and apply them to your life in the office:

▷ Use a number ("5 Reasons Why Memos Work for ABC Co.").

▷ Ask a provoking question ("Are you ready for Spring (Document) Cleaning?").

▷ Add alliteration or punchy concepts ("Documentation Nation is here! Ready to join the movement?").

▷ Add punctuation for drama ("The 6 Things We Need to Fix Our Information—That We're Not Doing").

▷ Make it a list ("15 Ways to Win Our Next Sales Call").

• **Use sentence variation—the long and the short of it:** Change up your sentence length to tell a great story. A short sentence has force. A long sentence can be beautiful. Then, *vary your sentence structure.* This is like moving your furniture around your living room to see what setup you like best. Take the sentences and paragraphs you threw down from the Capture and Structure phases and play around with the order. Use your eyes and ears to judge. The simple technique of playing around with the order needs no fancy training or writing skill. Shuffle and sort to give your story flow, build-up, and rhythm. Consider these two introductory sentences:

▷ The first line of *Moby Dick*: *Call me Ishmael.*

▷ The first line of *A Tale of Two Cities*: *It was the best of times, it was the worst of times, it was the age of wisdom, it was the age of foolishness, it was the epoch of belief, it was the epoch of incredulity, it was the season of Light, it was the season of Darkness, it was the spring of hope, it was the winter of despair, we had everything before us, we had nothing before us, we were all going direct to Heaven, we were all going direct the other way—in short, the period was so far like the present period, that some of its noisiest authorities insisted on its being received, for good or for evil, in the superlative degree of comparison only.*

Avoid Legalese and "Yoda-ese"

Dynamic writing may mean unlearning what you learned in college, law school, your CPA training, or (heaven forbid) your MBA. Use plain, concise wording and steer clear of verbose language. Replace longer, bloated words with shorter words. Short words like love, hate, best, or win are examples of power words. *Endeavor* is weak. *Try* is powerful.

"Henceforth, we will furthermore proceed with the proposal." Do you need to sound like you're in court? (Unless you are a lawyer, you don't.) Any word that doesn't add value lessens the impact of your document. Take it out. Be ruthless. Look for your inner Ernest Hemingway. His work had high impact and low word counts. It is said he wrote for easy understanding by those reading at a fourth-grade level.

While a junior documenter might try to sound important by using words like "bifurcate," a dynamic documenter makes concepts simple and digestible. Buzzwords, acronyms, and insider terms do not make you sound brainier; they annoy your reader.

I was reading a technical accounting article one morning when my three-year-old came downstairs at 6 AM wanting to read his book, *The Couch Potato.* I realized then that the best place to find inspiration for clean, clear language is within children's books. They use short, impactful words that sound pleasing, and they rely on powerful verbs.

Steal the Sizzle from Copywriters

I didn't even know what copywriting was until a writer mentioned to me recently that my writing "needs copywriting." I had to google it.

After one Udemy course and a stiff chaser of research, I realized that copywriting was something I had been sorely missing for too much of my career. You don't need to be a marketer to use these tips. Everyone should learn copywriting, whether you are an accountant, engineer, or plumber.

Write using "you" language. Not "XYZ Company wants to collect ideas." But "Do you have an idea to share?"

The copywriter's secret language is WIIFM (What's in it for me?). Your readers don't really care about your memo, report, or business case, or your product or idea, for that matter. They care about themselves: their jobs, advancement, looking good, and ROI.

Grab your reader by the ego. Write in the language of WIIFM.

Write Frequently

Don't wait for bouts of inspiration to find the opportunity to write. Hammer the keys or put pen to paper regularly. Use your smartphone's voice recorder or "notes" function to capture on-the-go inspiration.

Your brain will figure out most of what you need to do. If you use the steps of Dynamic Documentation, you'll never start with the proverbial "blank page." You'll start with the information you've captured, and a basic structure you've set in place will give you a strong foundation.

A lot of people think, "I'm not a good writer!" No one is born a good writer. I am not a good writer, either. But what I am good at is getting things on paper fast. I spew things out to get going. (Remember the power of the brain download to get the process started in the Capture phase.) By getting something on paper, however ugly or messy it might be, I discover what I know and what I don't know, which often leaves me leagues ahead of where I started.

Remember, too, that the more frequently you write, the better writer you will become. In James Clear's bestseller *Atomic Habits*, he quoted a fascinating piece of research. A photography professor divided his class into one group who would be graded on their quantity of photos and another group upon the quality of photos taken. Now guess which one had the better quality, overall? The ones with the higher *quantity* of photos. Why? Because they took more.

You may have negative memories of essay writing from your school days. They stressed me out, too. I transferred from the public school system to a strict private girls' school, Havergal College (which looks a bit like Hogwarts) in Toronto in grade 10. To my horror, a standard drill in many of my classes (English, history, and social studies) was "timed essays." This is where we were given a subject and then had an hour to write a short essay on the topic. How cruel! I was so far behind the other girls that I had to practice timed essays many nights after school.

To this day, I am indebted to Havergal College for this torture. This skill has helped me immensely. I never became one of the best timed essay writers in the class. But I did learn to work faster and with decisiveness. In today's distracted world, teaching the "timed essay" is an even more important skill as it gets more and more difficult for people to focus. You may think the art of essay writing is lost in today's world of free-form writers. True, we are more liberal with paragraph format than we used to be, but the fundamentals are the same—have a purpose, engage your reader, support your points, and conclude.

Turbocharge Your Language with Smart Writing Tips

I am not going to rehash everything you learned from English class or your technical writing course or the many writing resources out there. I have handpicked these tips, which are the most neglected in business writing and will improve your documentation immediately.

- **Cure "Noun-itis":** Noun-itis is a disease that infects business writing. Its symptoms are puffy nouns appearing where healthy verbs should be. If you have spent time in the corporate world, you have already been exposed, if not infected. (If your *specialization is the provision of documentation solutions,* get yourself checked out by a healthcare professional immediately.) Look at these verb-derived nouns. *Do they creep into your writing and choke it, like kudzu?*
  ▷ Performance
  ▷ Transformation
  ▷ Optimization
  ▷ Evaluation
  ▷ Solution
  ▷ Enhancement
  ▷ Production
  ▷ Execution
  ▷ Decision

Noun-itis masks what you mean. Worse, it's contagious. Accountants, lawyers, management consultants, and big corporations are the worst super-spreaders. Those afflicted with Noun-itis spread it subconsciously through their attempts to sound more "professional." An *evaluation* is less threatening than your boss *evaluating you*. *Reviewing solutions* is less threatening than *solving a problem*. *Making a determination* is less threatening than *we've determined*. You will be exposed to Noun-itis daily in meetings, through corporate reports and memos, and through attending conferences and seminars. The condition requires ongoing screening. Build up your antibodies through editing, proofreading, and practice.

- **Swap adjectives and adverbs for nouns and verbs:** You ask, "What is the cure for Noun-itis and text heavy with modifiers?" Words such as performance, evaluation, execution, and enhancement all have verb forms. With reconstruction, your sentences will be built back better, with strong, vital verbs that communicate action, proactivity, and strength. Look out for mutated verb forms (*-ment, -ism, -ure, -ness, -ity, -ence* or *-ance*, and *-tion* or *-sion*). Think of the verb to replace this and then rewrite your sentence. For example, does this activity *incredibly improve* your sales, or *boost* your sales? Is it *a cutting-edge technology* or *a game changer*? Our language is rich with power verbs and nouns. The right verbs and nouns pack a punch. Use verbs and nouns to take over from lazy adjectives and adverbs.

- **Get to know your online thesaurus:** Ah, but how to find the right nouns and verbs, you ask? Your thesaurus in Word is limited, but a quick Google search gives you free, high-powered alternatives. Your online thesaurus is the ace up your sleeve for finding the words that do the trick. Pick key words that you want to be stronger, especially verbs and nouns. Then use your online thesaurus to make them stronger, cooler, and more fun. I understand how daunting this all can be, for I have the habit of overusing the word "great." I need to stop myself before sending emails with twenty *greats* in them. Ask yourself, "Is the modifier necessary? Or even synonyms such as glorious, outstanding, commanding, and illustrious?" Be ruthless.

- **Punt the passive voice:** The passive voice is a plague on business writing. It is everywhere. It isn't unusual that I pick up a procedure or process and can't figure out what the heck it means with sentences like "the report is reviewed." (By whom? How? When? What?!) The passive voice is writing in which the subject is the recipient of the action. For example:

  ▷ Passive voice: "The wedding dress was tried on."

  ▷ Active voice: "Cindy tried on the wedding dress."

  The passive voice is an easier, sloppier way of writing because a documenter can mask their writing in obscurity. But to meet the Clarity, Re-Performance, and Engagement Standards, a dynamic documenter needs to weed out passive voice with a vengeance. Need a quick secret for hunting it down? Under the "Grammar" function in Microsoft Word, click on the "Passive Sentences" option to find those little devils.

DYNAMIC DESIGN

Documentation is inherently visual. You are literally taking information from thin air and turning it into something you can see.

We are programmed to measure our experiences based on visual presentation. Fine dining tastes better than food slopped on a plate (even if they do have the same ingredients). And you wouldn't wear sweatpants to a gala (even if they were more comfortable). How your documentation looks influences how people feel about what you are saying and how you conduct your work.

Dynamic design is about using visual concepts to get your message across and getting it to pop. There are no rules that say your documentation can't be fun. Here are some guidelines to help you.

Simplicity, Functionality, and Screaming Your Message

Your document needs to be legible and easily absorbed. Let your reader gain the gist of your document from your headers, bullets, tables, layout, and simple graphics alone. Let them grasp your content without doing much reading.

Be OK with white space in your documents, presentations, or sites. Remember that a strong, simple layout has more punch than a busy one. Focus on simplicity. Your message should stand out, not your design. Again, form follows function.

Like you did with your writing, you can start with too much. Strip it down later, in the editing or review processes.

By the way, if you are looking for design inspiration, look up the Bauhaus design school. Started in 1919, it's considered the foundation of modern design. It is the root of modern graphic design, too. The style is clean and slick.

Formatting (Too Much) Is for Losers

Microsoft Word is packed with formatting features. Don't go hog-wild using them just because they are available. It is one thing to know how to insert icons and funny headers. It is another thing to have taste in what you are doing. Practice restraint! Resist strange graphics that distract. Taste is a subjective matter. What appeals to some may be off-putting to others.

As a documentation person, I probably should have a strong opinion on fonts. I am not a fan of Times New Roman (because I used it in my horrible first jobs) and Comic Sans looks corny, but beyond that, I don't lose sleep over fonts. It should be readable, and it should not distract. Not too big and not too small.

Serifs versus sans serifs? The world's graphic design gurus are of mixed opinion on this one. A serif font (e.g., Garamond, Georgia) has small strokes or extensions at the end of its longer strokes, while sans serif fonts (e.g., Arial, Gill Sans, Helvetica) don't. Some experts say that serif fonts are easier to read in printed documents while sans serif fonts are better on a digital screen.

There are books and courses on fonts alone. And movies as well (*Helvetica*, a 2007 documentary, explored the history of this font and the world of graphic design). I advise against racking your brain on fonts or on formatting (the next-door neighbor to Template Hell, in my opinion).

Dynamic design is about using visual appeal to solve your problems. It is not about belaboring fonts, spacing, and margins. Really, the size of your margin is not going to make much difference in solving your problem (but do retain your white space).

Use a Standard Grid

Want to know the deepest secret of graphic designers without spending five years in design school? Use a grid shape. (It's that simple, seriously.)

This means laying out your document in vertical and horizontal columns. Move the grid to different proportions along the vertical and horizontal axes, depending on what works best for your text and images. The classic book layout uses a one-column grid. A magazine uses a multi-column grid structure.

A grid is not a cage. Without a grid, there is chaos and mess. With a grid, there is cohesion. It gives you freedom to be creative with your document while keeping a clean, modern, and professional look.

Don't center your layout. Use the grid concept to position your content.

Now, there are more complex design concepts that graphical designers do use. One is the Fibonacci sequence that looks like a conch shell and is the basis of one of the mysteries behind *The Da Vinci Code*. There is also an X design and an S design.

If you want to do fancier things and learn more about this fascinating topic, I encourage you to read more about design concepts from authors like Sean Adams. But, for now, stay in the grid.

Create Design Harmony to Tell Your Story

Dynamic design uses visual composition to solve your problem and communicate your ideas through layout, imagery, color, and form.

Consistency comes first. You wouldn't use different fonts or margins for each page of your document. (This would nauseate your reader.) Adopt some consistency in your visual layout from page to page or slide to slide.

Variety is also key. Most of us have favorite foods, but we wouldn't want to eat them three times a day every day (although my husband would make the exception for fries). Not every page of your document needs a piece of smart art, a funny picture, a table, long text, or bullets. You may have a favorite design tactic (mine happens to be my beloved tables). But you need to mix them up to keep things interesting.

Add Dynamic Diagrams

Maybe you don't like writing or are working with a team of visual learners. Or perhaps you are looking to tell your story in a flash or at a single glance. If this is you, use a diagram to communicate the information you need to talk about—data, processes, people, systems, controls, and more.

A diagram is like a painting: It is conceptual. I have picked up many diagrams that are too complex or busy, where the diagrammer believes they need to show every detailed step. Like a good painting, an artist must be selective in the details they choose to show or leave out.

Let's also get unconventional about diagramming conventions. There are a few standard shapes and symbols you will find in Microsoft Visio or other diagramming tools. But don't obsess over having the right shape or any of the other diagram rules. Dynamic diagrams are not about the protocol for diagramming shapes (this is another path to Template Hell). And don't take courses on this, either. They are a waste of time if you're not being hired for your graphic design skills.

The trick with diagramming is to train your eye and your gut to tell the story. Then test your diagrams with the Clarity and Engagement Standards to see if you are telling the story loud and clear. As complicated as some consultants may have you believe it is, process and data modeling aren't rocket science. Kids are naturals at it, drawing pictures of themselves walking to and from school (processes) or talking to their friends and family (data flows) or playing with their toys (use cases).

The fundamental concepts of process and data modeling are simple. Here are several powerful and accepted formats:

- **The swim lane:** This format helps visualize processes and roles. A swim lane diagram captures the process participants in their respective "lanes."

Swim Lane Diagram

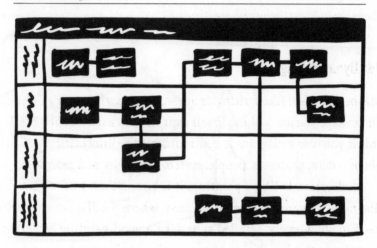

- **Data flow diagrams, with system inputs and outputs:** Use simple input and output diagrams for visual context inside larger documents. They bring clarity to how information flows.

Data Flow Diagram

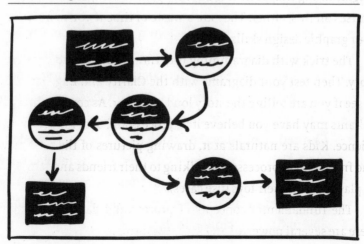

- **Use case:** A use case shows the interactions between a user and a system. This format is useful if you are a business analyst, software engineer, or designer.

Use Case Diagram

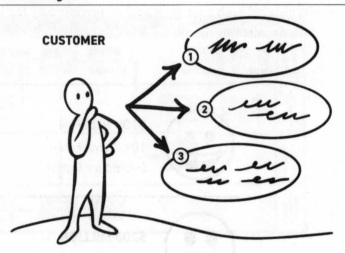

Add Surprise and "Pop" on a Shoestring:

There are a variety of readily available graphic design elements and tools that can make your documents shine. These include:

- **Screenshots or snips:** Let your Snipping Tool (by Microsoft) or competing tools like Snagit be your new best friend. I use my Snipping Tool all day. Snip images and plunk them in your documents. If you are building training materials, grab screenshots of how a user can navigate and use the system, tool, or spreadsheet.
- **Canned templates:** Programs like Canva have predesigned templates that are easy for non-designers to use. You don't have to be an Instagrammer either to benefit from the many ready-to-go designs for presentations, resumes, reports, posters, and much more available in Canva or similar tools.

- **Simple icons:** Don't be afraid to use basic icons, even to convey complex concepts. My company was once preparing a board presentation for a major company. They were evaluating several different financing strategies. Each option was nuanced. At the end of each option, we decided to use an emoticon to communicate how the client believed each strategy would be perceived by the investors. It looked something like:

Simple Icons

$200 MILLION
10% Convertible
Debenture Option

$200 MILLION
$15 Equity Option

It turned out to be a brilliant idea!

- **A dash of SmartArt:** SmartArt (by Microsoft, which you can find in PowerPoint or Word)—and I suppose other canned or preset graphics or shapes—can get a bad rap. I realize it isn't the most sophisticated of design tools. Dynamic design is about stealing secrets from designers, but it doesn't mean being too good to use easy tricks. SmartArt (or similar easy tools) can give your documents a focal point and can help you emphasize a point. Use SmartArt as you would add spice to stew. Enough for flavor, without overwhelming the dish.

- **Simple tables and graphs to communicate number values:** Use simple graphs to communicate information faster than numbers in a table format. Microsoft Word, Excel, and PowerPoint all have wizards to create graphs in a matter of minutes. Which one can you read faster?

Tables and Graphs

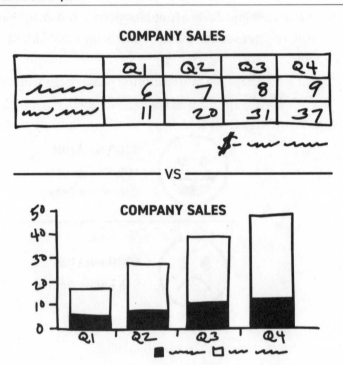

COMPANY SALES

	Q1	Q2	Q3	Q4
～～	6	7	8	9
～～	11	20	31	37

—— VS ——

- **Stock photo your way to creativity:** There are so many cool stock photo sites that you can use to make your SharePoint sites, presentations, documents, and even emails have more pop. I once built a template library for a client in SharePoint with humorous stock photos for buttons. My client was so happy and engaged by the images that the picture buttons got more attention than the hundreds of documents that I created behind them on the site! Trick your client or boss into seeing you as highly creative just by finding the right pictures. Some free pictures can be cheesy and low quality—you don't want to use those. Spending a bit of money on the right images can go a long way to making your materials memorable.

You've captured vital information, structured it, presented it in a compelling fashion, and are now charging your way toward the end zone. You and your team have developed a set of fundamental Little d skills that will propel you to bigger results to solve your documentation problem and achieve real-world results.

It's time for perhaps the most daunting phase of our work: How to communicate what's in your documents to share your work with others and strengthen it through feedback.

CHAPTER 6

Communicating

What gets shared gets put into action.

Why is "Communicating" part of Dynamic Documentation? Because communication makes organizations smarter. And a smart documentation practice radically improves communication.

Putting aside all the experts, books, and topics on communication, the definition of communication is, in fact, very simple. Communication refers to:

1. The exchanging of information.
2. A means of connection between people.

Let's focus on the first part of the definition. Documentation has everything to do with exchanging information. Dynamic Documentation excels at exchanging information with *purpose, clarity,* and *power.* Documentation also serves the second definition, since it connects people by getting them to a common understanding and moving them in the same direction.

We could also add a third definition: Communication is about persuasion. Verbal skills and the confidence to deliver messages convincingly are critical for being a good communicator. Documentation is an overlooked part of communications in the corporate world. Documentation allows you to communicate your thoughts even if you aren't in the room. (Of course, it is better to be in the room, too, but you can only be in one place at a time—documentation expands your reach.)

Don't put documentation on a pedestal. Make it come to life. The most important point you should gain from this chapter is that documentation *must* be shared—whether in meetings, on paper, in presentations, or through any other form of reporting. If you aren't going to share and communicate it, why are you wasting time on the documentation in the first place?

Let's go back to your specific documentation challenge. Symptoms of communication challenges include:

- Documentation is created but no one knows about it.
- Documentation is kept in silos and not shared across the company.
- Lack of sharing leads to rework and starting projects over.
- Documentation is never "good enough" and doesn't get shared.

Most of us are familiar with corporate communications in the form of contrived emails or postings on our corporate intranet that deliver the tone at the top from company leadership. But "Big C" corporate communications and other initiatives often fall short of the true essence of communications—building connection between people. Your Big D project needs a strong foundation of Little d skills of sharing, listening, and rebuttal to get your team working together at their collective best.

4 PRINCIPLES OF DYNAMIC COMMUNICATION

To understand the connection between communication and Dynamic Documentation, let's look at these key concepts:

1. Dynamic Documentation Is Built to Be Shared

Unless you are creating purely administrative or CYB (cover your butt) documentation, or your documentation is solely for personal use, documentation is created to be *shared*. Don't just go through the motions. If you aren't sure or can't see the point of sharing the information, then ask yourself why you are working on the document in the first place.

2. Documentation Is Meant to Connect with People

Dynamic documenters are excellent communicators; documentation and communication skills are tightly linked. By communicating with the people around you, you are creating a culture that shares and values information. You are building an environment that leaves strong information behind when you move on from a project. You are making sure others get the benefits of your work. Some examples:

- Emailing your meeting notes to confirm what was learned by the team
- Engaging with and showing the team a draft of your work
- Making your documentation accessible (e.g., emailing, SharePoint folders) to your team or other people in the company
- Taking time to ask people how your document looks and whether it suits their needs
- Sharing your notes to help someone who was confused in the meeting
- Using your document to help someone new to their role, especially if they are struggling with a new system or project

3. Communication Is a Two-Way Street

Documentation depends on a continual feedback loop. Documentation must capture information and then vet this information and communicate the findings back. The process is circular. Dynamic communications flow both ways. Think of communication as a flow of information, intellectual capital, and brilliant ideas coming in and out of people and into the organization. Dynamic Documentation is the vehicle for serving this communication flow.

As a consultant, I am constantly capturing information by talking with people, responding to them, or engaging in a meeting to reiterate and capture some more. But it is not just about the collection of information. Dynamic Documentation engages a collective dialogue to resolve the issue and think of better paths forward. Think again of the interviewing skills of talk show hosts.

The Capture and Communicate steps are opposite sides of the same coin. Capture is about collecting what you need for documentation. Communicate is about giving the information back to team members and out to other stakeholders.

Dynamic Documentation separates Capture and Communicate into distinct steps to emphasize their distinct purposes. But in the real world, these steps blend with and bleed into each other.

4. Communicating Involves Risk

Communication puts you in a vulnerable position. It's OK to be wrong sometimes—own it and embrace it. Being a communicator and a documenter is like asking someone out on a first date. There is the potential for rejection or disappointment.

So why bother? Like dating, communication is necessary for advancement. Without communication, your organization, career, and life in general will stagnate. "If you're to have a chance at succeeding, you have to stay excited in the face of failure," says Stanford Electrical Engineering Professor Emeritus Martin Hellman, the co-inventor of public key cryptography (i.e., that uses pairs of keys—public keys and private keys).

Though it is often hard to push through our resistance, *it is far better to be "wrong" about your stance on certain topics than to just let your ideas, thoughts, or comments die.*

If your articulation or analysis has flaws, or for some reason your idea can't work, the documentation process, through its natural feedback loop, will find those problems. The process will make you better for it. Being clear and driving your team to have a better understanding of the topic is more important than being right.

Even when you are wrong, you find this out fast. That is better than carrying wrong information for the whole project—or your whole career, for that matter.

As a consultant who "sticks my neck out" to get things documented, I have been wrong many, many times. The work world is often confusing. Meetings are not well run, even in the best of companies. People often don't give you the right answers. Jennifer will say something that conflicts with Raj that may conflict with Cindy. You can't avoid it. This is part of the process.

People don't document or communicate enough because they fear being wrong. But let me reassure you, after taking meeting notes *thousands* of times over the past fifteen years, I can recall *one* time where I was scolded for my interpretation of the conversation. The criticism came from a not-very-nice, soon-to-be-former client.

The point is, the flack you will take will be rare, at worst. Suck it up. It doesn't hurt that much, seriously. It's worth the risk.

DYNAMIC MEETINGS

I could write a whole chapter on how to improve meetings. Yes, they should have a purpose, put a value on people's time, stick to a time limit, include only the people who should be there, and on and on. There are a ton of resources out there on best practices for meetings, if you are looking for more information.

But Dynamic Documentation brings something extra to the table. The practice keeps you keenly attuned to which meetings matter, and which are a waste. And furthermore, dynamic meetings are an opportunity to seize ideas, action items, and follow-ups. Like a rabbit, your ears are perked up, listening for information you want to turn into intellectual capital, which will add more value for the organization and yourself.

In terms of actual "documents" that support meeting presentations, here are two approaches to consider, among many others.

To PowerPoint or Not to PowerPoint?

If you have been in the business world for some time, you have probably developed a certain opinion on PowerPoint presentations. PowerPoint is dominant in many meeting cultures. In recent years, there has been a bit of a PowerPoint backlash because of rampant overuse and too much time spent on "perfect" presentations with little substance.

It's hard to disagree. I have seen teams spend all week preparing an update presentation for leadership, only to begin work on the next update meeting right after the last one ended. I have sat through many horrendous presentations at training sessions or conferences where presenters put little thought into what they were going to say and invested all their energy on fancy and sometimes hard-to-follow slides. I will admit to getting sucked into a PowerPoint perfection trap myself.

I am by no means anti-PowerPoint. It has its place, especially when you need to give structure to what you are saying or when you want your audience to see your words. Other times, it helps you keep the group focused and put boundaries around the discussion. PowerPoint can also be a blessing for remote meetings.

During COVID-19, when my work world was remote, PowerPoint became my quarantine friend. When you are on a call with a large group, you have no idea if people are listening, and I like the fact that it can give a record of what I said.

When using PowerPoint, you need to guard against the perception that it's a one-way form of communication. It is not totally PowerPoint's fault, truth be told, but that's the way it is often used. If you are using PowerPoint and want to practice the art of Dynamic Documentation, make sure your presentation builds in a way that encourages two-way communications. Otherwise, your audience will just sit back and watch you present.

Visual Facilitation

I first read about "visual meetings" from David Sibbet's book of the same name, and I eventually took one of his graphical facilitation courses at The Grove Consultants International in San Francisco. Visual meetings directly contrast with the one-way style of PowerPoint.

Sibbet's concept of the visual meeting is about adopting a cool cartoon style of icons and images to draw the discussion in real-time on large wall-sized pieces of paper. There are a lot of ways to create what are often called "facilitated" meetings (aka "lean" sessions or "graphical" facilitation sessions). This is a popular area in the realm of business analysis and is used by some consulting firms as well.

A great facilitator, specifically a "graphical facilitator," captures the audience's thoughts and creates memorable notes. Bringing visual concepts to meetings doesn't need to be fancy or time consuming. You don't need to hire an expensive facilitator, either. You can build basic visual concepts into your meetings with a few simple ideas, such as:

- Drawing out a few agenda items on the whiteboard (e.g., a bull's-eye for a target, a lightbulb for an idea)
- Creating a meeting agenda to visualize the topic, such as a simple SWOT (strengths, weaknesses, opportunities, threats) matrix
- Giving team members sticky notes to add ideas to the whiteboard

The important thing to keep in mind is that the purpose of a meeting is communication, not one-way reports, jockeying for status, or face time. If you keep your focus on new ideas, alignment, gaps, and actions, you'll get much more out of the meetings you attend and the meetings you lead.

DYNAMIC EMAIL

Some of you may read this and say, "Email? Is that still a thing?" I know it's not the newest or the hippest tool out there. And it faces its share of criticism: too much spam, too much time suck, and can't we just have a meeting?

But I disagree. I love email. It works for me. Email spans our new-school and old-school ways of working and thinking. Email, or essentially our Microsoft Outlook suite, brings all Dynamic Documentation concepts (i.e., Capturing, Structuring, Presenting, Communicating, Storing and Leveraging, Leading and Innovating) together in one tool. It is a distillation of the whole documentation process. You may never write a memo or use a SharePoint site, but you can exercise all the skills and concepts of Dynamic Documentation through your email practices alone.

Dynamic email isn't about rules around how to use email (or the broader Outlook suite). Your use of email depends on your role, relationships, and personality. No two people use it the same way.

Dynamic email is about understanding and contemplating the different dimensions that email plays in your documentation toolkit.

Email Can Save You Time (Yes, I Said Save Time)

One study estimates that the average knowledge worker spends three hours a day on email. Anti-emailers argue that email is too much of a time suck.

I would put myself above that three-hour average, but I disagree that it is a waste of time, especially if you treat email like a craft. Why? Email updates, follow-ups, and iterations of a work in progress (not mindless chains) get me out of meetings and phone calls, which I would argue *are* a time suck (or vortex or abyss, for that matter).

It may sound antisocial to send an email when you could pick up the phone or book a meeting. But depending on the number of projects or clients on your plate, you can't be on the phone and in meetings all day, or you wouldn't get anything done.

We all need "briefings" to stay on top of what is going on in our projects, operations, or businesses. Email lets you stay in the know.

To be a dynamic documenter, you need to work smart. To work smart, you can't be stuck in firefighting mode all day, every day. Sure, you will have to fight fires from time to time. But addiction to this way of working (and yes, it is addictive) will hurt your cognitive processing—your ability to be creative and effective—over time.

Dynamic email is a more reasonable in- and outbox than your texts or chats. Think of it like walking over to someone's inbox with a piece of paper with a task to do. You wouldn't hand them a crumpled ball. Dynamic emails are thoughtful and less knee-jerk than your texts.

If you are struggling with staying on top of your emails, the one and only "rule" I recommend is the *24-Hour Rule*, which we discussed in the Capturing chapter. A 24-hour window gives you a rhythm to your email responses that is respectful to your team or clients, keeps you on track, and unchains you from your inbox. While I typically respond in less than 24 hours to most emails, I still use the 24-Hour Rule to give the right balance between focus on non-email tasks and not dropping any balls.

Email Is IP, But Text and Instant Message Aren't

Text and instant message are like one-night stands. Email is a long-term relationship.

Text and instant message may be good for one-off communications like "Can you make the 3 p.m. meeting?" But email creates information that you can leverage for future work. It creates a trail of burgeoning intellectual property (IP)—the ideas, insights, and breakthroughs you and your organization are generating. Or should be.

You can mine email. You can save it. You can use the almighty copy and paste.

A large part of my consulting business is taking information from conversations and turning it into action. Email is often the conduit to make this happen.

Email Lets You Stay In Touch

Are you old enough to remember writing letters to your friends and family? Maybe you had a few pen pals, like I did. I can remember buying writing paper and stickers, doing little drawings for my friends and family, and adding pictures to my letters.

You can still put the *mail* back in email. Think of using email to pen pal with your business contacts, old people you worked with, your family, whoever. You may use other tools these days (such as Facebook). But the concept of keeping in touch is a dimension of email that shouldn't be lost.

Email is the most old-school of the new-school technologies. It is a lot like traditional letter writing and even feels a bit like it. You will give letter writing its modern email spin, I know. But don't let the corporate world and the bad habits take away from the potential, even beauty, of letter writing.

Reach out to others in the company. Reach out to past clients. Reach out to others you have worked with in the past. You may be surprised how powerful this tool is, to this very day.

Email Creates a Record Keeping and Audit Trail

I have a confession that is going to shock my friends, especially those who are lawyers. I don't track my billable time, even though billable hours are how I make my living. Documentation drives behaviors. When I have tracked detailed hours and daily billing in the past, it has led me to focus on very short-term goals at the expense of longer-term goals.

Dynamic email records what you are doing and gives you a paper trail. My email is how I record my billable time. Every time I work on something, I will send the client or my staff member a note. If I have gone to a meeting, I write back. If I have reviewed something, I will summarize with an email. If I have been planning, I will email to the team what I have planned.

I was once working with a large audit team where I was in the habit of copying my boss on my interviews, interactions with others, and review notes. She told me I was the only one in the entire department who communicated what I was actually doing.

Using email to conclude the task or a logical step allows a clean break before you move to the next activity you are working on. It allows you to say "done," at least for now.

Email Sets the Tone of Your Relationships and Shows Your Personality

Email plays a large part in our relationships with our superiors and staff, our peers, and our business associates and friends in the industry. Each email embodies the hierarchical relationship between sender and recipient. Tone matters.

We use email so much in our business lives that it has effectively become an extension of our personalities. Some say that curt emails are impolite. Think about context, though. If you are an investment banker (or other "red" personality, as we call them), maybe your peers write like that, too. Being curt (read: brief, without frills) and efficient is how you want to reflect your personality or fit in with the crowd.

If you run a dance studio, writing with exclamation marks and smiley faces might be "on pointe," as they say. Don't be afraid to add personal style to your emails. It's OK to use creative punctuation, emojis, or stock photos if they help you to let your personality shine through!

Consider these three styles of communicating the same response:

1. **Will do** → You are quick, efficient, and no-nonsense.
2. **Will do.** → You seem like a formal or more traditional person.
3. **Will do! Thanks.** → You are friendly and excited.

I worked with a woman who was a nice person, but her email tone came across as rude and accusatory. This made it difficult to bring her into projects. On the other hand, I once hired a writer whose email personality was phenomenal. So much positive energy and fun, with a quirky stream-of-consciousness style. You feel like you are really talking to her through her emails and getting a glimpse at what she is thinking. Needless to say, the last time I tried to hire her, her schedule was booked for more than a year with client projects.

Email is tricky at times. You may innocently word your message in a way that can be misconstrued (or "misheard") by the reader. Let email reflect your personality and the tonality of your organization. And always be alert to how your words will be interpreted by your reader.

Email Is a Better Influencer Than Social Media

There's a reason you still get flyers overflowing your recycling bin. Mail—whether physical or email—converts.

Book marketing experts such as Tim Grahl, author of *Your First 1000 Copies*, and others are unanimous. Email outsells social media. We have an intimate relationship with information that comes into our mailbox whether we want to admit it or not. It screams, "You need to process me!" and elicits connection and action.

I was once having difficulty getting any traction on a communications tool that my client needed. We had been talking about this for months. So, I threw the idea into a structured email to the organization's vice president. The idea got instant traction after that. I didn't need permission to write a formal memo or business case. Everyone has permission to email.

Email is a vehicle to sell your ideas. This is where human psychology comes in. Your ability to sell concepts through email, among other channels, will accelerate your career overall and your ability to make an impact.

When using emails to sell, small changes in formatting have a big impact:

- Leverage the power of the subject line. An email with "Re: Re: Re:" in the subject line has less chance of being opened than one that starts: "Important New Business Lead."
- It's OK to have a long email. If you have lots of points, put them at the bottom of the email and separate from the message.
- Unless you are asked to do a formal memo, don't use an attachment. Just paste it into the body of the email. You will have a better chance of the email, and your valuable information, being read. Not to mention, many cybersecurity systems will punt emails with attachments and send them to "email purgatory."

So, check your email attitude for a day, a week, or forever. Consider these new truisms of email and then plan ways you can make email work for you.

DYNAMIC REPORTING

If you are a consultant, handing in regular reports on your work may be a normal part of your job, as it is for me. And I get that, if you are an employee, you may not always have the same formal opportunities. But just because your role doesn't call for formal reporting doesn't mean you can't "report."

By reporting, I'm not saying "writing someone up." I am referring to updates that offer conclusions, summaries, or recommendations. There are lots of situations where you can practice reporting without formally calling it that:

- Writing a "lessons learned" or "best practices" document for your project
- Summarizing the pros and cons of a new corporate training program
- Providing recommendations in a memo about a new process or product
- Reporting on the status of a project or task

Dynamic Reporting is a type of documentation that is about sharing ideas, driving decisions, summarizing work performed, recommending a course of action, or giving information to someone more senior than you. But don't limit how you think about it or rack your brain with the definition

Dynamic Reporting

Reporting gives your work a history.

Reporting shows guts.

Reporting drives better work.

DYNAMIC REPORTING

Reporting gets ideas out and into action.

Reporting ensures you use verbal communications appropriately.

here (whether you call this a memo, analysis, update, communication, presentation, or whatever).

Reporting is about actively communicating a message, problem, vision, plan, or summary. It is about anchoring your analysis, work performed, or thinking by committing it to writing.

So, why should you report?

Let's explore.

Reporting Shows Guts

Reporting shows guts. It shows you aren't afraid to draw the line in the sand and take a position. This will very quickly differentiate you from the rest.

Try this Dynamic Documentation secret to improve your reporting immediately: Write yourself a "What's Working and What's Not Working" memo.

"What's Working and What's Not Working" Memo

This means reporting out at a point in time to voice your opinion about the project and to determine next steps.

Choose anything you are working on and give this task to your team. You can use full paragraphs, point form, or pictures. Whatever. The point is that you are saying what you think. I use this approach with my team as we craft reports for clients. It is a remarkably powerful tool for cutting through the noise to conclusions and to drive us to what we ultimately need to communicate.

Reporting Gets Ideas Out and Into Action

At the beginning of this book, I mentioned that the tools in this book aren't meant for Amazon. Well, it turns out I was wrong. Despite Jeff Bezos's reputation of being cutting edge, even prophetic, in his business decisions, it turns out he uses a dynamic—yet totally old-school—documentation practice: the memo.

To get their innovative ideas across, Amazonians don't do fancy Power-Points (Bezos hates them). They write old-school memos explaining their ideas. Amazon team members sit in silence reading the memos before team meetings and, after everyone has read them, the team discusses them. What a great system! Why? Reporting is an equalizer. Introverts and extroverts get equal opportunity to share their great ideas this way. The process reduces the importance of grandstanding, fancy graphics, and one-way communications by shifting the importance to analysis, thinking, intelligence, and ideas.

Reporting Gives Your Work a History

Reporting is not just about sharing ideas. It is about bringing your work to light. You can do the greatest work possible "in the field," but your budget or project will get cut if you have no connection with management or the board. Dynamic reporting gives your work legs.

Reporting gives your work or project a searchable history, tracking what has been done, key ideas, conclusions, and other important information. Don't be one of those employees or consultants who leaves a trail that is too hard to follow (or no trail at all). Assume your report will be the only thing people will find after you have left a project, a role, a client, or a company. In the case of many of the audits or analysis projects I run, most of the documentation that supported the project is never referred to again, but the reports are almost always revisited.

In my Internal Control business, I have implemented a rigorous process of reporting to our clients' managements and boards. As a result, these clients have grown accustomed to and even addicted to ongoing reporting. These clients have stuck with us for the long term largely because of reporting that gets the visibility of senior management and the board. If we didn't have these reports, our work and our accomplishments would be forgotten.

Reporting Drives Better Work

Through my many years of reporting, I have learned that a strong reporting practice is not only good for the client, but also good for me—and specifically my ability to deliver the best product. Reporting solidifies information and gives you better feedback. I start working on reporting early in my projects, not when fieldwork is done. This process forces my team members to be clear on what we need to dig for.

For most projects, you can keep digging deeper and deeper into the details literally *forever.* This is a challenge for my audit and accounting coworkers and staff because they love the details. Early reporting, which is like a later-stage of the brain dumping we learned in the Capturing step, is enormously effective for drawing a line in the sand on what you are thinking, what information is "good enough" for now, and where you need a bit more.

Reporting Ensures You Use Verbal Communications Appropriately

Our company once started work with an international energy service company that was afraid to put any audit or Internal Control issues into writing. The previous Director of Compliance was deeply worried by the idea that the company was going to "get sued" or "get in trouble with the regulators" (concerns which were unfounded, in this case).

Management and the board of this company were used to hearing that "everything is awesome." Once we began to commit work to paper, "the rubber hit the road," as they say, and in this situation it turned out that things were not as perfect as management once believed. But we could at least now look reality in the face and make meaningful changes and improvements. The bottom line? You are *miscommunicating* if you are using verbal communications inappropriately (e.g., verbal board updates instead of written reports).

Regular reporting gives you power and helps manage the narrative. Be sure to seize that power and use reporting to your advantage.

What is the next step in Dynamic Documentation? You've captured needed information and structured it. You've honed your ability to present your knowledge and insights in the most compelling fashion and learned how to use dynamic, two-way communication to share findings, iterate, and get the most value out every meeting, conversation, and event.

Your team and your organization now have processes, reports, memos, and visuals to help them to see the path forward.

And next? You need both a place to put your documentation and a retrieval system for quick and easy access.

This next step is Storing and Leveraging, which explores how you work with documents that are "done" or are "out there" in your organization. This is where the value and utility of your documentation will grow exponentially.

Save it once;
reuse it often.

CHAPTER 7

Storing and Leveraging

I t is ironic that there is so much talk about "information overload," and yet we are overloaded with information about this overload. Of all the topics in this book and in the world of Information Management, the subject of documentation storage is the most discussed. Just look at all the courses and articles on enterprise content management, content management, and similar topics.

Storage is important. You absolutely need a place to put your documentation and a system so your documentation retains and grows in value over time. But it is just one piece of the picture.

"Leverage," however, now that's the big payoff. Leveraging (which is more commonly referred to as "maintaining" or "monitoring") is about driving value out of your documents over the long term. Leveraging is about reviewing your documents, document system, and related processes to make continuous improvements, and then harnessing this information to effect change.

Here's a quick litmus test to see if your organization has a storing and leveraging problem:

- No one can find anything. Ever.
- Documents are stored all over the place with no structure.

- You have a ton of outdated documents, and the updated documents are hard to find.
- No one owns or is accountable for your existing documentation.
- People store important documents on their own computers, not where they can be easily accessed by others.
- There is no process for storing, maintaining, and updating documents.

The Storing and Leveraging step teaches us concepts that span our Big D (e.g., system implementation, information governance) and Little d (e.g., organizing our files) worlds. Your Little d common sense around concepts like systems and what to store (or not) will save you big Big D dollars, time, and resources on your next enterprise solution or Information Management program.

While Storing and Leveraging comes toward the end of the 6 Steps, every project begins with storing. At the outset, when you start capturing information for a new issue or project, you set up a place to save and share your work. Even if you never embark on a major, system-wide cleanup or documentation review, you can begin each new project on the right foot, and you'll see the benefits right away.

Let's get started, but first, a brief "around the world" tour of a few terms under the Information Management umbrella to avoid any confusion and get you up to speed. While these concepts are not described explicitly, they are embedded in storing and leveraging best practices:

Information governance

This is an umbrella term that refers to the rules for information and for following up on these rules. In practice, this usually means there is a team or someone responsible for setting the rules (i.e., policies, procedures, practices) and then making sure these rules are followed (i.e., through audits, reviews, interviews, assessments, and monitoring).

Metadata

Simply defined, metadata refers to "data about data." When I was growing up in the eighties, I remember using manual index cards (also called the Dewey Decimal System) in the school library to locate books on the shelves. Those manual index cards were a form of metadata. Today, metadata is stored in databases, and the concept is pretty much the same as it was back in the day.

Classification

Classification systems are a means to categorize your documentation. We do this all the time, whether we are organizing our house or our work lives. You might have an area in your closet for "work" clothes, for "house" clothes, and for "gym" wear, too. In systems, we achieve classification through various means, like metadata, folders, navigation structure, and security features.

Content management systems

Content management (or related terms like document management, records management, and email management) systems are like filing cabinets but with advanced tools for entering the storage and finding your information.

Workflow

This is the concept of moving documents through a process, typically involving other people. This might be the approval of contracts or expense reports, hiring new staff, making purchase orders in a procurement process, and so on.

Access to content

Access design allows the right people to retrieve your content. Role-based security protects your documents from the eyes of unauthorized people. Access design considers issues such as confidentiality and privacy of the information.

While Information Management may not be officially in your job title or part of your job description, we all have the responsibility to capture and disseminate documentation. Dynamic Documentation, particularly as part of the Storing and Leveraging step, is about stealing the secrets of Information Management and information governance professionals and making these concepts accessible to everyone.

If you are looking for more information on the Information Management topics listed above, I recommend you go to AIIM (Association for Intelligent Information Management) for reference materials. You might also want to learn more about technologies that dominate our landscape today, such as Microsoft SharePoint, Microsoft Teams, Dropbox, and Google Drive.

10 BEST PRACTICES FOR DYNAMIC STORING AND LEVERAGING

As we have seen throughout the 6 Steps of Dynamic Documentation, everything comes back to common sense, which often means taking Little d skills and smart thinking to maximize our Big D project value. It's about deliberate design. Focus on these key concepts to get even smarter about problem-solving and documentation practices for you, your team, and your organization overall.

1. Methodology Trumps Technology

When you go to fix your documentation problem, the first question you might ask is: "What technology should I use?" As humans, we cling to the belief that tools will solve our problems. Organizations continually implement the latest and greatest tool, hoping to dramatically improve their documentation and processes. This often results in discovering their "foolproof" solution is full of empty promises and is destined for failure (and obsolescence).

I have watched companies implement fancy tools for projects, audits, and Internal Control programs only to realize that email does the job much better with *zero* configuration. I am embarrassed to admit how many tools I have tried for our business that have failed miserably. I once spent months playing with an app from my personal trainer, only to revert back to emailing her my progress.

10 Best Practices for Dynamic Storing and Leveraging

1   Methodology trumps technology.

2   Get a handle on your "infoflow" before automating your workflow.

3   Create great documents before thinking about storage.

4   You need fewer documents than you think.

5   Action beats perfect systems.

6   Information is made to be shared—today and tomorrow.

7   Store once, use many times.

8   Separate active and finished documents.

9   Separate or discard "trash" documents.

10   Information needs an owner . . . or at least someone who cares.

Yes, we do need structured apps for high-volume activities like incident management or purchasing. (And of course, I'm an advocate of useful tools and streamlined systems that can give us scale, repeatability, and control.)

But don't get too misty-eyed when the next vendor approaches you with a utopian system for your business, at least for most areas. Focus on the process and your business needs first. Find a solution with the tools you already have on hand: It might be your email, the whiteboard in your boardroom, your team's shared folders, your SharePoint or Teams sites, or your notebook.

Technology on its own will not clean up your files, systems, folders, or even fix your metadata. And solutions don't just happen through the work of magical little elves. Access, configuration, settings, changes, training, testing, troubleshooting, and support are not to be taken lightly. Before you buy a fancy new tool, weigh the high cost of fiddling.

Get your process right before the platform and invest in scale when the ROI is clear. This is true for your personal tools and systems, as well as your team's, and of course enterprise-level investments.

2. Get a Handle On Your "Infoflow" Before Automating Your Workflow

Workflow has become the engine of the corporate world and the superconductor of our knowledge-based economy. However, the workflow I am talking about here isn't SAP or Oracle, Six Sigma or total quality management. I'm talking about our human ability to "flow" work—or "infoflow"—which is a far more interesting discussion.

Storing and Leveraging may be the Biggest D of Dynamic Documentation, but like everything else we have learned so far, it is the Little d application that can break Big D's back.

Before you implement an automated workflow for you, your team, or your organization, get a handle on your infoflow first.

Your personal infoflow is about recurring sources of information throughout your workday:

- Meetings
- Ideas
- To-dos
- Notes
- Projects
- Folders
- Customers
- Issues
- Sales opportunities
- Information requests

Your team or department has infoflow of its own through a range of activities (some of which may not be necessary after all):

- Meetings
- Approvals
- Shared files
- Forms
- Project management tools
- Tracking systems
- Chats (electronic, water cooler, and other)
- Memos, processes, and reference materials
- Decision-making records

Think of yourself, your team, or your department as an information processor. What information goes in and what comes out? Draw a diagram of your "flow." My personal diagram would show people talking to me (inputs) and me spitting out documents on the other side (outputs). A team diagram should show team meetings, files, systems, and workshops going in one end and your "product" (sales, closed orders, proposals, completed work, etc.) out the other.

Visualizing your team's or department's infoflow is your first step to improving it. Ask yourself if your inputs (i.e., meetings, notes, discussions, systems) are leading to better outputs (i.e., what your team is designed to do and deliver) or is the correlation murky to say the least? Are your interfaces designed with world-class simplicity (like Google)?

3. Create Great Documents Before Thinking About Storage

I once had a client who had trouble with their request-for-proposal (RFP) documentation. Their management decided to go out and buy costly new RFP software. This purchase got them nowhere. After the system was implemented, they realized their real problem was the quality of their RFP and marketing content. They had RFP documents that didn't resonate with potential clients, so, who cared about storing them in a sophisticated and pricey new system?

Creating great documentation always comes first. Content is king. Focus on storing, retrieving, and safeguarding *only* documentation that is high quality and adds value to your team or company. By value, this could mean making the company more money, training staff, and also CYB (covering your butt) on matters of compliance, regulation, or financial considerations.

Once your team shifts its focus toward creating smart documentation, you will find documents will become easier to store and maintain. The reasons for this include:

- The documentation becomes more important to your team.
- People keep the documentation handy and regularly use it as a reference.
- Departments or teams now share your documentation to help clarify points.

I had a meeting a few years ago with a tech company that had developed a tool to help organizations find and classify a variety of files across various formats and departments. The president of this tech company admitted to me that it was only the well-constructed, thoughtful (I would say "dynamic") documents his clients really cared about. Finding "a lot" of documents through this sophisticated new tool didn't seem to matter. It was only the few good ones (that probably never went missing in the first place) that did. Quality, not quantity.

4. You Need Fewer Documents Than You Think

Channel your inner Marie Kondo. Before I developed a more mature approach to my own personal documentation systems, I would go through my yearly "get organized" ritual for my home office, and the first thing I would do was rush out to Staples to buy a new file folder holder, in-basket, or other document-organizing contraption. As a result, I now have piles of these collecting dust in my basement!

I need discernment about what information I keep or don't keep in my life. Even though documentation is my specialty, and I touch thousands of documents a year in my work life, I have come to realize I don't need all that many documents in my personal or even work life. In fact, I don't need much in terms of organizing tools at all (which is why my previous Staples purchases are collecting dust).

I recently performed a "deep clean" of all my reference paper materials when I moved offices. After touching thousands of materials from clients, conferences, courses, presentations, and other activities over the year, there were only four (four!) paper records I decided to keep. These documents were the only ones that met my criteria of: would be used for future reference, were current or not time sensitive, and were not available online or in softcopy. I quickly scanned these four documents and shredded the other papers.

In her *New York Times* bestselling book *The Life-Changing Magic of Tidying Up*, Marie Kondo describes storage experts (in the context of home organizing) as "hoarders" because they focus on storing clutter and not discarding it. *How true in our work world, too!* Only our storage solutions in the work world get much, much more expensive and confusing. Marie Kondo's thinking has significant Big D impact, too. If you apply the thoughtful discernment stressed throughout the book, you may find your organization needs to keep far fewer documents than you think.

Applying discernment to your documentation is critical for the following reasons:

- Most documentation has a shelf life. Documentation should be created to drive action. Once that window has passed (either the actions were completed or not), the documents start to lose their value or become outdated.
- Much information is available online these days. You don't need to store nonproprietary information.
- Most documents are not critical, and many are useless.

How many pictures on your phone are actually valuable to you? How many of these pictures would you miss if you lost them? How many of them would you pay money to keep and protect? (Most of the pictures on my phone have been taken by my five-year-old, for example.)

I wonder how many CEOs or managers are rushing out to buy new (much more expensive) storage solutions before doing their spring-cleaning and before stepping back and looking at the pictures they keep on their phones?

5. Action Beats Perfect Systems

You might think your team has a problem with storing documents. You might blame your system, or the quality of your documentation, or your folder structure or metadata.

Experience has shown that the real culprit is usually a failure of the basics. It's the little things, like daily, ongoing upkeep of your documentation, that will bring your storing and leveraging process down. How your team handles the documents, information, or ideas that pop unannounced into your day in 24-hour spurts is where you find the gold. Remember the 24-Hour Rule. People need to act on things in 24-hour windows. Examples? Dealing with a lease renewal, processing an invoice, processing notes, responding to emails, or editing a document.

━━━▶ The Action-Over-Perfection Protocol ◀━━━

states that documentation systems and practices should
be designed around driving action and changing outcomes,
not around perfect files, metadata, or configuration.
Documents and documentation systems that drive momentum
are more valuable than "perfect" documentation.

Use the 24-Hour Rule, the Personal Productivity side of the Documentation Triad, and your Little d discipline to get your team's documentation on track. Get your team to work in daily and weekly increments, and then implement regular documentation reviews to keep them on track for good.

6. Information Is Made to Be Shared—Today and Tomorrow

Sharing is not a fluffy concept. I get that your company has information marked "Private" and "Confidential," but most information—for Dynamic Documentation purposes—should be shared as much as possible.

You, your team, your department, and your organization need systems and practices that ensure your information is easily shared. This is a place where better tools, such as SharePoint sites, Teams, Google Drive, Dropbox, or others, can improve the ability of your information to have more leverage.

I once found a large amount of brilliant training materials in a client's files. The problem was that no one knew about them. What a waste. By adding a few easy buttons in SharePoint, I made the training materials readily accessible to everyone in that department. Sharing is about enhancing awareness of these valuable materials.

Sharing doesn't just mean for today. Think about the future. When the Apollo program ended in 1972, the factories that assembled those vehicles were re-tasked or shut down. The technicians, engineers, scientists, and flight controllers moved on to other jobs. In the process, we lost our blueprints. We can't get back to the moon without serious reengineering.

7. Store Once, Use Many Times

Use the mantra "Store once, use many times, and build workflow around documents." This concept comes from the Information Management world and is a practice well worth the time. It will reduce duplication and make the management of your documents a heck of a lot easier.

In Information Management circles, you may hear the related and equally excellent term "single-source publishing." Single-source publishing is about having the same content used in multiple ways and across multiple platforms and media. Whoever is creating or updating the document (e.g., process, policy, communication, memo) only needs to do the work once. The source document can be stored in one place and reused.

Here is a simple example. Many of us email documents, sometimes many documents, back and forth to team members to get them reviewed. Email increases the risk of one of your team members using the wrong version, or forwarding it to unauthorized personnel, with the risk going up as the document volume increases.

- First level of solution: Instead of emailing, email a link to the folder.
- Now, let's get to the second level: Store the document in SharePoint or a similar tool. SharePoint lets the document be shared easily and provides version control.
- Let's take this example to the third level: Instead of emailing the document, you build a workflow around the document. This "forces" the document to go through the levels of review or approval. You wouldn't do this for a one-off. But it's smart for a series of routine documents such as purchase orders, personnel records, approvals of expense reports, or even policies or processes going through levels of review. The point is that documents live in one place, but the workflow forces them to go to other people for review. Some companies find this so effective that they are taking away their shared drives.

8. Separate Active and Finished Documents

Is your storage scheme no better than a musty old attic crammed with rarely reviewed artifacts from decades past? I picture Indiana Jones movies in constant reruns on TV.

Archives are historical documents about a place, institution, or group of people. In the Information Management space, archiving is about moving documents into the archives and out of the more expensive, higher-capacity work-in-progress area.

For Dynamic Documentation purposes, I want you to take a broader look. Think of archives as documents that you are "done" with. If you are looking at a mismatch of works in progress, half-done, old, and outdated documents all lumped into the same folder structure, you are not alone. This is common. If your documentation problem is about not being able to find things, there is a good chance you are struggling with this concept.

Separating your active and finished documents is an easy "quick win" that will give your team the immediate benefits of:

- Visibility into the status of projects in progress
- Clarity in understanding which projects are closed and the final documents delivered to clients or other stakeholders
- A more formalized project close-out process, where documents must be transferred to the archived or closed project folder
- More visible reference material through clearly marking the finalized/closed projects and documents
- Cheaper IT or physical storage in certain cases: Archived information is typically cheaper to maintain than documents sitting in your more precious work-in-progress space. You wouldn't use up your expensive downtown office space to store rooms full of paper records. (I remember this practice vividly from working at TD Bank in the 1990s—boxes of documents being shipped from the expensive downtown King and Bay Toronto real estate out to storage in the 'burbs.)

9. Separate or Discard "Trash" Documents

Unless you have been living under a rock for the last decade, you know organizations are faced with a massive amount of information. This trend continues to rise exponentially in a world hungry for more data. Organizations are faced with siloed tools and systems. They have massive duplication within and across repositories. Everyone is keeping everything forever. Storage is cheaper than it ever has been, and this intensifies the issue.

"ROT" (redundant, outdated, and trivial) documents are your "trash" documents. As well as separating your "archived" files from your "works in progress," you need to also pull ROT documents from your file or your current projects. ROT documents creep up through previous versions, outdated contracts, and people storing things two, three, or four times.

You may choose to weed out your ROT documents during or at the end of a project. This is an ongoing process, where you need some consciousness to delete or isolate these documents (e.g., I often use a ROT folder to avoid deleting something I shouldn't).

The Compliance, Governance and Oversight Council conducted research into the nature of information in organizations. They found that 70 percent of information was ROT. This survey was conducted some years ago, and our junk percentage is growing. I would not be surprised if it is closer to 90 percent sometime soon.

10. Information Needs an Owner . . . or at Least Someone Who Cares

Strategy in place, the next issue is: Who shall be responsible for this storing and leveraging process, and be held accountable for results? There needs to be a "throat to choke," as they say. Maybe two.

In your company, the responsibility for creating new documents or document systems may be clear. But responsibility for storing and leveraging could be a different story. It is not uncommon that I walk into a company or team where no one really knows who is responsible for existing documents, managing what's on their drives, or maintaining their Share-Point sites.

Task someone to take responsibility. That person should be empowered and their authority communicated. You could rotate the responsibility among squad members to see who does the best job. You need to find that person who wakes up in the morning thinking, "How can I improve our organization's documentation today?" (Seriously, that's the thought that gets me out of bed in the morning.)

In Information Management circles a few years ago there was a utopian vision of enterprise-wide projects for larger companies in which teams across individual companies would share and document in perfect harmony. There is currently debate around even "trying" for enterprise-wide projects for larger companies. For some clients, the vision of getting all organization data into the same platform or system and having all teams coordinate in perfect harmony is too lofty a goal, at least for now. Other than the technology challenge, it boils down to an accountability problem and a compensation problem. Departments are not always rewarded for sharing with other departments.

THE HOW-TOS OF STORING AND LEVERAGING

In practical terms, for each project or issue, you can follow these simple storing and leveraging how-tos to get the most out of your work.

Set Up Your Document Storage Scheme at the Beginning of a Project

This may take you as little as 20 minutes (for smaller projects). These 20 or so minutes can go a long way. I have learned from many past mistakes when I didn't take the time to set things up at the beginning.

Organize your files based on:

- How people will be working on the project
- How people will use your documents, files, and systems
- Logical categories (e.g., by process, document type)
- Consistency across your projects
- How you will ultimately report on the project
- How the final deliverables will look
- Quality priority ("best in class": the best documents in a particular stage come first)

Choose an Information Hierarchy

Using a best-in-class "framework" is a good way of setting up folders for certain types of projects or initiatives. For projects, the Project Management Body of Knowledge (PMBOK) is a great framework to get you started (while the methodology is weighty to read). Focus on the core PMBOK concepts:

- Initiation—business case, project charter
- Set Up the Project—project plan (including sub-plans, like communications plan, cost management plan, quality plan)
- Execute—working files, actual project deliverables
- Monitor and Control—steering committee slides, risk management, and change management documents
- Project Close—lessons learned

Bucket and "Split Out" Documents at Project End or Critical Juncture

Cleaning up your documents will be the last thing in the world you want to do at the end of a project or long assignment. But "bucketing" and "splitting out" your documentation is how you get real power (aka leverage) out of your documents for the long term. It's time to step back and separate out your documents using the best practices we talked about above.

One director I worked for had the foresight to give me about two weeks' budget (which is a rarity) to do a thorough document review for a major infrastructure project we were closing off. From this review, we split the documents into the following buckets:

- **Garbage:** There is no way we will use this again. (Move to ROT file.)
- **Reference:** This is good reference material. (Moved to Closed Project file, read-only for reference.)
- **Template:** We can reuse this material as a template for new project. (Moved to team's Template Library.)
- **Working Document:** These materials are part of the living materials. (Moved to the operational teams' working folders and sites.)

It turns out that those two weeks of cleanup paid off big time. The documents and templates we moved into the team's Template Library supported the operational teams and were used on many other projects, too.

Conduct Audits When Appropriate

Like an Internal Revenue Service audit (but without the anxiety), a documentation audit looks at evidence and tests the necessity of documents or supporting data. Audits (at least in theory) should rely on "hard" evidence (e.g., documents, logs, screenshots) and not anecdotal evidence (e.g., interview results, feedback surveys).

Consider using audit concepts in your documentation review practices to:

- Pull documents or evidence to support a finding
- Support your numbers or work performed with documentation

- Look for "hard" evidence
- Question any areas where evidence is conflicting
- Get external objectivity from your team or department (where possible)

Conduct Annual Reviews as Part of a Compliance Initiative

Over the last few decades, the corporate world has been hit with a perfect storm of regulations and compliance standards—data privacy laws, the Freedom of Information Act, the Health Insurance Portability and Accountability Act (HIPAA), the Payment Card Industry Data Security Standard (PCI DSS), and Sarbanes-Oxley (SOX). Regulations mean more documentation and they also mean a requirement for an annual review. I have talked about the dangers of documenting because "you have to" and how this often leads to Stage 3 documentation—that is, documentation that is jammed down your team's throat because of reasons like "the auditors said so" (my personal least favorite) with no connection to its actual value.

But as I have grown in my work and as I have lived through harsh economic downturns, I have grown to appreciate mandatory and quasi-mandatory projects. Regulatory programs give you a lever to pull when all other levers are gone. The budgets for these programs may get reduced but are not cut as quickly as discretionary programs (e.g., optimization, business process reengineering, change management). So, use your compliance programs or regulatory and other mandatory programs as an opportunity to add value through improving your documentation and "looking under the hood" at least once a year.

Build in Nonmandatory Review Cycles as "Preventative Medicine"

I have heard that doctors and psychologists are paid close to five times more money to deal with patients in crisis than they are to keep patients in good physical or mental health. This is true in the documentation space, too. We neglect the basics of staying on top of our documentation. And then, when we see that nothing is working, we rush out to bring in a costly new system, team of consultants, or restructuring experts after things have gone wrong. Regular updates and audits save you time and money in the long term. A proactive cycle, updates completed iteratively, and small improvements over time (without needing to spend a lot of money at once) lead to lasting success. Many of the best practices we should build as habits in our organizations are the same as those mandated by regulatory projects:

- Regular process updates
- Checking documentation against defined criteria
- Pulling evidence (i.e., like an audit procedure)
- Reporting to management
- Making continuous improvements each year

Conduct "Unleashing" Reviews to Purge, Refresh, and Get a Clean Slate

Think of a documentation review as an opportunity to unleash the power of your collected information. This style of information review is proactive but informal. You may go into your team's files naturally if you are a manager (although you might be surprised that I have worked for many who don't). Maybe you are having a brain-dead day in the office on a Friday after burning the midnight oil on a project (or, hopefully, something more fun) the night before. Maybe you are looking for ideas or inspiration. Maybe you have (don't say this too loudly) some downtime before you start your next project.

Unleash the good stuff (e.g., the brilliant training materials, killer presentations, thoughtful analyses that your team did) and let it into your work. Kick the bad to the curb.

You've got bigger fish to fry. Specifically, optimizing your ability to lead and innovate.

CHAPTER 8

Leading and Innovating

> *Documentation as a subtle, but powerful, form of influence.*

L eading and Innovating is like a bonus step of Dynamic Documentation. It is about taking everything you have learned in the previous chapters and now pushing them one step further.

The hallmark of a leader is their ability to influence people. Influence is not a grandiose or negative thing. Influence is the ability to improve someone's understanding, thinking, and, ultimately, actions.

Leadership means you are looking to the future. The evolution of documentation practices is part of this (both exciting and challenging) future. You need innovation to make the little improvements to your team or organization *and* to make the game changers. Dynamic Documentation frees you and your organization to become a change agent in today's rapidly changing world. You'll wield new levels of impact, engagement, initiative, energy, and organizational citizenship.

Leadership and innovation go hand in hand. If you are a leader in your organization, you need innovation. If you are an innovator, you need leadership skills. Documentation skills are catalysts that connect the two.

Your documentation problem has to do with leading and innovating if:

- You struggle to balance your company's old ways with the realities of the new world.
- Your team is having the same conversation repeatedly with no forward movement.
- Your team clings to an old documentation model that fails to elicit new ideas or encourage the modernization needed for success.
- Your team is going through the motions on their routine documentation.
- You cannot attract people with a documentation mindset to work for you.

Success in today's environment, including success with your Big D projects, requires a different kind of leadership and innovation. It's not enough to lead by authority. It's not enough to throw in a new tool. You need Little d thinking, instincts, mental makeup, creativity—and all the tricks you can muster—for your team, department, or organization to win at its next big project.

In my days at business school, and at many conferences I have attended over the years, there is the underlying assumption that climbing the ladder is the only route to a rewarding and lucrative career. That is far from the truth. I have been a consultant for many years and have worked many long hours. But I have never and probably will never get to the title of manager.

Let me tell you that you can have an interesting, fulfilling, and financially rewarding career—and be a leader—from a different dimension (without climbing the ladder that is often greasy and missing some rungs). Dynamic Documentation allows you to give your organization's brass the intelligence they need to make the decisions that make things happen.

If you are the person who takes the meeting notes, you filter what is important or not. If you write the project plan, you are the one to influence task assignments. If you write the communication, you control the message. Documentation is a subtle but powerful form of influence.

Dynamic Documentation gives you superpowers to spot issues, unstick projects, speed up work, and make whole teams and organizations smarter, faster, and better. When you use those skills and habits on a consistent basis, in formal and informal ways, you get noticed and make a difference.

UNRESOLVED ISSUES—CONFRONTING THE GROUNDHOGS

We have talked about leadership being about things like momentum, initiative, decisiveness, and decision-making. This all sounds nice in theory. But your grand plan for being an outstanding leader in your company will be thwarted by what I call "Groundhog Day" issues or "groundhogs"—named after the 1993 movie *Groundhog Day*, in which Bill Murray plays a man who must relive the same day over and over again—if you don't know how to deal with them. You know what I mean if you have ever:

- Been in a "Groundhog Day"–type meeting and could swear you had the exact conversation the week before
- Heard the same topic discussed in about ten different ways by ten different people across your company
- Felt an eerie sense of déjà vu at work

If you recognize any of these experiences, I feel your pain.

Groundhog Day issues infest our organizations. They are one of the worst sources of wasted time and energy—even worse than today's distraction of social media. If your team talks about the same topic over and over and over and over and over again, it will leave them unproductive, demoralized, lethargic, unmotivated, lazy, and ineffective.

Groundhogs are everywhere in our corporate culture, no matter the size of your company and no matter your industry. They are everywhere in the public sector and academia, as well as in large organizations and small private companies. Groundhogs invade our homes and our personal lives. I have seen groundhogs running amuck in pretty much all organizations I have worked with, and I will admit to having a few in my house, too.

- I have heard the same discussion from the same external audit firm (no joking) about fifty different times.
- I have been to meetings about projects no one had the intention of kicking off at least for a few years.
- I have been to countless team meetings where half the meeting was just talking about Groundhog Day issues that were discussed the

week before and the week before that and the week before that and so on.

- I have talked about countless projects for my own business—better sales process, cleanup initiatives, new templates, website changes, newsletters—that have never (yet) happened.

I also have extensive experience in catching and exterminating ground-hogs. The good news is that, unlike Bill Murray's character who is stuck in the time loop in the movie, you can break free of Groundhog Day issues by using Dynamic Documentation tools.

The Groundhog Trap

involves using documentation techniques to stop runaround
conversations about future projects or past decisions.

Groundhog Trap

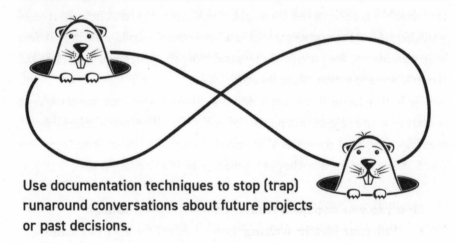

Use documentation techniques to stop (trap) runaround conversations about future projects or past decisions.

Groundhog Breeds and Techniques

I know from experience that groundhogs exist in one of two common breeds. Let's explore.

The first breed consists of projects, initiatives, to-do items, or ideas that are talked about, but never acted on. With no defined actions, they are the amoeba of ideas, without form or shape. They just float.

A second breed is made up of positions, stances, or decisions that an organization has made that frequently need explaining, re-explaining, or justifying. The goalposts move. The egg is never hatched. (Excuse these mixed metaphors!)

Ideas and projects talked about and never started

Most teams and companies have projects they have never started. People do, too (I have lots). It's OK to have things you are planning on doing—or at least *plan on planning on doing*, or even plan on *thinking about* planning on doing—that are not started yet. But it is *not* OK to let these ideas morph into ground-hogs. Even brilliant ideas can turn into groundhogs if you let your team talk about them too much. It is almost daily that I hear something mentioned that should have been a step forward but was just a step in a circle. Your team probably has ideas or concepts that just keep coming up in meetings. If they keep coming up, they are probably good ideas or things you should do but haven't. So, take action. Move forward.

By letting these issues turn into groundhogs, they become a negative impact to your self-esteem and that of your team. They waste mental space, meeting time, and resources that should be focused on moving areas forward. Worst of all, groundhogs become a terrible cultural norm.

How can you stop ideas from turning into groundhogs?
- **Put your idea in writing:** I once worked for a VP of Finance at a postsecondary institute who was pulling his hair out having the same conversation repeatedly about how the college should handle ancillary revenues. Should we allow bake sales? Can we allow the athletic department to do their own thing? How do we get our deans to agree? Whose job is it to manage ancillary revenues, anyway?

My client felt he was talking in circles about the same topic, and it was sucking him into never-ending meetings. I was hired to write a policy, procedure, and guidelines for how the college should handle ancillary revenues. The client's recommendation to create a policy, procedure, and business case were spot on. We created this set of documents in a couple weeks. While we didn't eradicate the groundhogs completely, we at least contained them by giving the college staff written guidelines to follow when they approached these scenarios.

- **Build a repository for ideas and action items:** Maintain a "parking lot" or a list of ideas and action items for yourself and your team. Treat this like a holding place for managing your great ideas. One of my clients used a tool to allow people to submit their innovation ideas through a *Shark Tank*–style concept. This was a great way to track and monitor ideas.
- **Put it in your calendar:** Put actions in your or your team's calendar to take them off your mind. (For me, this method works about 50 percent of the time, but it's better than not planning at all.)
- **Build a queue of projects or areas of focus:** Assuming that your team members are human (we will get to nonhuman team members in the next section), you can't give them unlimited projects and hope to be successful. Instead, build a queue of sorts for projects. With my Internal Control clients, I am upfront in the planning process about which areas of focus we are concentrating on each year and which ones we aren't. This is a queue that brings focus and practicality to what we can and cannot do each year.
- **For goodness' sake, stop talking about it!** Your documentation should have it covered. Make a commitment to stop talking about the idea unless you are really going to push it forward.

Decisions and stances that need to be re-explained

The second breed of groundhogs you will find rooting around in areas where no one knows why things were done a certain way. Here are some examples of potential groundhog positions, stances, and decisions you may see in your own organization:

- Decisions on why the company waived or enforced a requirement
- An accounting position for the company
- Reasons the company went forward (or not) with certain projects
- Positions as to why a company has adopted certain internal processes
- Positions as to why a company has adopted certain practices to support legal, compliance, regulatory, or audit requirements
- Decisions to spend more or less on one area

How do you prevent decisions from turning into groundhogs?
- **Hire a business analyst or someone with similar skills (if you aren't one already):** A good business analyst has the skills to interview, capture information, and drive results into something tangible. They should have strong problem-solving skills. These skills should kill these types of groundhogs (or, at the very least, humanely trap and release them back into the wild). Documentation is typically—or should be—fundamental to their work. Many of us do not have the title of "business analyst," but we function like business analysts. This includes pretty much every single one of my consulting projects in auditing, compliance work, policy development, documentation reviews, and process implementation.
- **Go back to the basics of interviewing and note-taking:** Note-taking captures the history of the decision or relationship in many contexts. (If you hire a business analyst or other associates, make sure they are excellent at note-taking.) I worked with an oil company that was operating "in good faith" with their IT service provider. The IT service provider did great work but, as the complexity of the oil company's business grew, it was time to shift the handshake deal to a formal one. I brought in an IT consultant who interviewed team members and the IT service provider,

reviewed existing documents, and gave me great notes that we easily converted to a report. Using this report, which documented the relationship between the oil company and the IT service provider, they entered into a formal arrangement only a month later. Without great notes to capture the history, the process could not have started.

- **Report, structure, communicate, and build a report people can use:** Go back to the technique we learned in the Structuring step. When you are handling this breed of groundhog, bigger, omnibus documents are the way to go. One large document is often the best way to explain a topic that has grown organically over time.

- **Circulate your document to contain the groundhogs:** Use the document, not the groundhog, to do the talking. I once worked for a large multinational on a SOX 404 project (SOX being post-Enron legislation mandating that US-listed publicly traded companies establish Internal Control programs). The company had taken a different approach to journal entries than you would typically see for a company of its size. Unfortunately, my client was burrowing a groundhog hole having the same discussions with their auditors every year. Worse, the external auditors (like all the Big Four accounting firms) had a high rate of turnover, which meant the issue would get explained and then re-explained again to new team members. When I started working with the SOX team, they had a "Journal Entry Memo," which described the company's control environment and why they have taken the approach that they did. (This was a sixty-page omnibus document.) This was a smart approach. I took over the role on a contract basis, updated the Journal Entry Memo, and used it extensively to fend off groundhogs that came our way (namely junior auditors). While I wouldn't say we ever got the auditors to "agree" with my client's approach, we could at least use the Journal Entry Memo to thwart an impending groundhog infestation.

DYNAMIC DOCUMENTATION AND THE ROAD AHEAD

Dynamic Documentation is, well, dynamic. That means it is changing, as documentation practices must adapt to our modern life. Videos and photos are more popular forms of image documentation than we have ever seen before. While we don't traditionally think of social media as a form of documentation, it certainly is. It is about documenting your life, brand, or intellectual capital, and then sharing it. I am not using a strict definition here, but I am suggesting we think more openly and liberally about emerging documentation and how we define it.

The shape and form of Dynamic Documentation will evolve with our changes in technology as well as consumer tastes and trends. On the same note, the basics of Dynamic Documentation are here to stay. It's no different than sales. The internet has changed the mechanics of selling, but it hasn't changed the fundamentals of sales, like solving the buyer's problem, branding, follow-up, and so on.

If you were to ask me if documentation practices are getting better or worse overall, I would say better, to a certain degree. Our business landscape is under more regulatory pressure than ever before. And our work culture is shifting to avoid "single point of failure" of our employees—that is, risking losing information when an employee leaves.

On the other hand, our workforce is stymied by distraction. This is hurting our ability to listen, capture, discern information, write, and get things done. Focus means a lot more than just staying off YouTube at work. We send tons of emails, and we bring our phones and laptops to meetings. We could be losing the personal connection with documentation we used to have. Social media has made everyone their own media empire, which has put new challenges on information control.

These circumstances and the associated needs for documentation will continue to change with the times, our work skills, and the regulatory and legal environment. There is a lot you can't change in this shifting cosmos, but you can at least adapt your documentation practices, systems, and mindset.

We need more Little d skills as part of this future—the skills that lead to more Big D corporate change, too. Going back to basics is a critical need in leadership and innovation today, not lip service.

Information Stresses for Modern Leaders

Legal risk	Lost institutional knowledge	iPhonization of documentation
Data growth		
Regulatory requirements		Security
		Distraction
Mobile workforce		Work from home
Job hoppers	Technology change	Hybrid work

Workforce Evolution . . . and Transition

Today's workforce is more mobile than ever. Pension plans are disappearing. Retirement at sixty-five with a gold watch has been supplanted by the gig economy. Institutional knowledge? What was that again?

In our transitory gig economy, the average professional is more of a free agent nowadays, moving from one job to another. The new age of job-hopping is one of the most significant influences on documentation practices. You can't just walk down the hall and ask "Bob" about the IT system he built for an insurance broker in Kansas City three years ago. Because "Bob" has now left for a new company (and manages IT for a hotel in Playa del Carmen). Or else he has joined the gig economy.

Companies now need documentation to train their staff on how systems, processes, and protocols work. Thinking of your staff as permanent fixtures is dangerous. Verbal communications are not reliable, and we cannot count on them to capture our precious intellectual property. Organizations need to capture and store their IP through solid documentation practices in systems that are cataloged and easily searchable.

How can you adapt to workforce changes?

- Plan for people suddenly leaving your team or your business.
- Document your people's knowledge through processes, memos, analyses, and desk procedures.
- Focus on production and output. While knowledge is nice, doing something with the knowledge is more important.
- Get active about reviewing where documentation is and how it is stored.

Automation

The rise of automation is real, but it's not the whole story.

McKinsey Global Institute (MGI) estimates as many as 375 million people around the world may need to change occupational categories and acquire new skills by the year 2030. You have probably seen the first wave of automation of simple tasks, analysis, and "bots" at play in your organization already.

The notion of robots coming in to take our jobs is scary to all of us. But many experts believe robots will change the nature our jobs for the better. Automation will displace many jobs over the next 10 to 15 years, but it will create many others and even more will change.

What is the role of documentation in all this? Let's take a look:

- **Documentation can detail the steps of a specific process:** If you want to automate a process, you need a good handle on it first—which means you typically need to document it. Some computers today can document their own code, which is making certain documentation a heck of a lot easier. But documentation doesn't happen by itself in most cases. I once worked with a small airline to deconstruct how they had built their homegrown booking and incident management system out of Outlook. The team couldn't automate until they knew how their existing system and supporting processes worked.

- **Documentation defines the scope and defines a large-scale, transformative change:** Let's say you have a vision of completely changing your company's operations and processes through a new system or series of solutions. You need to document this vision. You will need your dynamic skill stack (e.g., note-taking, document creation, writing, design, and storing) to execute on this vision. I once created something called a "Cash Culture" for a large multinational. This was a grand vision of putting cash upfront in their decision-making. The company needed to improve their systems to do this, but the systems were the easy part. The document needed to sell the vision first.

- **Documentation saves the cost of rework:** If you build a system but have no documentation of how the code works, how access was designed, or how the configuration and parameters were set up, please prepare yourself for expensive rework. I worked with an organization once that had spent a fortune on consultants to develop an enterprise resource planning (ERP) system. But they had a dispute with the consultants in the end and the consultants left no documentation behind. Using documentation practices, I worked with the client to pick apart the basics of how this system was designed (e.g., master data, access, role design, and workflows). Had the consultants left even modest documentation to explain how and why things were set up a certain way, it would have saved us a lot of rework (which, BTW, took us years to do completely).

- **Documentation gives legs and wings to change:** After automation, the world you work in will be different. Automation means thinking about different approaches to how you collect, create, and communicate information. Take a simple example. You automate data entry for your sales orders. What happens? You need to implement the change. Tell your team what's changing. Train your team members on how to handle sales. Now add the human back. Maybe your accounts receivable clerk has more time to talk with customers, handle issues, and run your collections process. Documentation plays a role in each of these steps.

Automation intensifies the need for better documentation more than ever. It will mean a worldwide shortage of Little d documentation skills. There's never been a better time for documentation. And for CEOs and entrepreneurs, automating processes by ensuring your documentation is in place can save incalculable time and money in all aspects of your business. Documentation and automation go hand in hand. It doesn't mean you are replaced. Your job is iterating as you speak.

Robots, in the final analysis, may allow us to be more human. Robots are taking over repetitive functions and freeing us for the jobs of the future. These require different skills—more Little d skills like thinking and feeling in the workplace.

Dynamic Documentation is not about reciting code or about storing reams of data. It is about making people's lives at work better. Only a human can do this. Only a human can help teach another person and have intuition regarding what information they need to look at, what sounds great on paper, what's useful, what's engaging, and what looks cool. I can't teach Dynamic Documentation to robots, at least not just yet.

How can you adapt to increasing automation?
- Develop your (human) Little d documentation skill stack of writing, communications, engagement, collaboration, and psychology.
- Have a personality. Breathe personality into your documentation, too.
- Learn to sell. Selling doesn't mean knocking on doors; it means getting your point across.
- Lead and innovate. And set yourself apart from machines.

Communicate, connect, and create. A robot will never beat you at that. (Hasta la vista, baby.)

iPhonization of Documentation

The Romans were dynamic—and exceptional—documenters. They kept records on every citizen. And they documented every trial, law, and announcement. To create their first-class documentation, the Romans used papyrus scrolls (from the papyrus plant) or parchment (made from animal hides).

Today, information, or documentation, lives in emails, blogs, data, chat lines, and system audit logs. These new forms of data are challenging traditional documentation practices specifically around storing and leveraging. How do we classify this information? How do we locate and capture it? How do we store it? How do we update it? What has privacy or confidentiality concerns (e.g., is a chat subject to concepts like privilege)?

Civilizations have always needed systems for managing their information. Like any civilization, we need to change with the times. But our "civilization" today is global. So, together across the world, we are coming up with better methods, technologies, and practices to rise to the challenge.

The iPhonization of the world as we know it has shifted our technology to focus on the user—on what we *want*, all the time. This has created new challenges and opportunities for documentation practices.

In our personal lives, we are thrilled by so many cool toys to choose from. (This brings its own challenges, as you know.) But once we get to work, we wonder: Where are our cool toys? Where is our exciting user experience? Why is our work world still focused on documentation practices that seem lifeless and disengaging?

It is no wonder the word "documentation" is disliked, or even scorned, by many in the corporate world. (This applies to all generations, by the way.) Our out-of-touch documentation practices are just another reason today's workforce is getting increasingly distracted and disengaged. How can we focus on work when we are carrying with us a portal into unlimited and interesting content and games?

The corporate world has a long way to go when it comes to keeping up with the fun toys in our pockets. Unlike my generation, the generation now entering the work world grew up with smartphones, being entertained all the time by technology, and ordering whatever they wanted online; a great user experience has almost always been a part of their lives.

The tools for documentation need to change and evolve to keep up with users and their personal lives. Here are just some areas that are ripe for change:

- **Smartphone synchronization:** Documentation practices are becoming more and more synchronized with our smartphones, allowing immediate upload and download from the cloud. New documentation tools must allow users to connect their documentation processes (uploading/downloading pictures, making approvals, reviewing materials, and so on) increasingly to their phones. Ten years ago, only fancy firms had access to sophisticated information tools. Today, these barriers have eroded. I can now access all my files from my phone, which is awesome when you are running from client to client.

- **Photo documentation:** Since we all carry cameras, picture documentation is increasing dramatically, with no end in sight. In the Internal Control and Internal Audit world, photo evidence is becoming more popular and acceptable with millennials and Gen Zers shaking up a pedantic profession. Photo documentation will become even more accepted and normal for the next generation accustomed to using photos over paper or other written text.

- **Video documentation:** While video documentation is used extensively for training, there is no reason the application shouldn't expand to other applications, including audit documentation and recording meetings. The first time I ever saw myself on video, I was twenty-three years old working one of my first jobs, and the company hired a corporate trainer to videotape (that's what we said back then) us to improve our presentation skills. Compare this to my kids, who have known how to steal my phone and look at videos of themselves since the age of one. The generation entering the workforce grew up glued to video (starting with their parents' phones and iPads), and the use of video will become a more normal part of corporate documentation, too.

- **Animation documentation:** Why stop at just video and pictures that we already use? The next generation is looking for even more stimulating toys—consider documentation that can be edited through animation practices. Animation has been used for construction and interior design for some time, but the application will extend across process documentation and myriad other areas. The cost of animation is not high. I have hired a cartoonist in the past, too (though not a full animator), and the pop and value you get is incredible.

- **Virtual reality and video gaming documentation:** Virtual reality and video gaming technologies have been used for things like military training and teaching pilots how to fly. But again, the application will continue to expand with the next generation of gaming lovers—just think of the possibilities for improved user engagement. I have clients applying virtual reality to training in oil and gas, construction, and the retail sector, too.

- **An avalanche of cool new apps:** Like many business practices, there will continue to be a slew of new apps that will make documentation more engaging. The trick here is to test them and remain adaptable to the new app options to support your documentation practices. Expanding your digital mindset—and not locking yourself into one or two apps or platforms—will become key over the next century. It's a hard balance to avoid getting overwhelmed by the new apps, too.

- **AI (artificial or augmented intelligence):** I am admittedly short-changing this discussion. AI is an enormous, exciting field, and we are only just starting to feel its headwinds in our work world. AI is about having a computer mimic how your brain solves problems and makes decisions. It ranges from the automation of simple tasks to driverless vehicles, with everything in the middle being game right now. AI and other automation trends like blockchain will change our documentation practices in many ways. Investment in AI for communications, for example, increased significantly with COVID-19.

I watched even my less techy clients move to more sophisticated AI tools that tailor their messages to their specific audiences, rather than blaring out the same content for everyone. This is a radical shift in corporate communications—from a one-size-fits-all model to a nimble, tailored, Instagram-era, dare I say "dynamic" approach. AI will change documentation practices for audits, design, engineering, manufacturing, and many other areas, all with a push towards intelligent content. By complementing AI with Dynamic Documentation, you can make your work more than just intelligent (i.e., able to learn); you can make it smart (i.e., able to make things better), too.

- **Disappearing documents:** You are almost finished reading this book, and now I'm telling you that documents are disappearing. Yes, in an old-school sense, they are. Let's take a couple simple examples. ABC Co. implements an integrated, real-time ERP. What happens to their old ways of receiving invoices from vendors, circulating approvals, mailing checks by snail mail, and entering transactions by hand? In ABC Co.'s new environment, these transactions work in real time. Vendor invoices are replaced with online submissions, approvals are routed, payments are transferred automatically, and journal entries write themselves.

  Take another example. XYZ Co. replaces its physical engineering drawings with 3D computer-assisted design (CAD). What happens to their plant and engineering drawings and manual markups? XYZ's engineers edit the 3D CAD models through the software, and XYZ Co. doesn't need as many large drawings lying around its office anymore, nor the stress of managing manual markups. Documents are disappearing to make way for a more integrated, real-time, and data-driven world. But fear not. Documents are only a construct for how we interact with information. Data and Dynamic Documentation skills will morph and expand dramatically over the next few years. Documents will disappear, but documentation certainly won't.

How can you take advantage of digital trends and technology?

- Take advantage of the tools that you have already and use them better over time. There's a lot of hype around digital adoption nowadays, but it's not as intimidating as it sounds. Digital adoption is about taking a consistent approach to improving your organization's use of its technology through regular feedback from users and stakeholders.

- Experiment with Microsoft product suite tools. I am trying to be technology agnostic, but Microsoft products are ubiquitous and also powerful. They also have a lot of impressive and popular features that are easy to use, such as Forms, Lists, SharePoint, Teams, or Visio.

- Experiment with different tools and learn from your failures. While I am not the most tech-savvy person I know, I do experiment with tools for my business. I have bought many that have not worked out. While I start with the best intentions, I often realize that I have picked something far too complicated, and my use of the tool usually just doesn't go that far. But at least I keep learning and advancing (albeit not as quickly as others). It's a work in progress.

Dynamic Documentation can't just be "this month's consultant-driven initiative" or the CEOs latest "bee in the bonnet."

To succeed, there must be ongoing commitment, all the way from "Capturing" to "Leading and Innovating." Because it's all of a piece. We need to capture (sniff out those truffles) and process information in a way that is usable and easily accessed by the right people, then merchandised internally to leverage its worth. Doing so finally frees the organization to do its best work without fear of failure and criticims—the glide path to breakthrough profitable growth and innovation.

Whew! I know; that's a lot. But I think now you're ready to begin that journey.

Now let's take a look at how all the pieces come together so you can put Dynamic Documentation into immediate practice in your work—and in your home life as well.

PART
3

Dynamic
Documentation
in Action

Change begins
one action
at a time.

CHAPTER 9

—

Applying Dynamic Documentation at Work

T he tips we cover in this chapter are intended to help you take the Little d concepts you learned and apply them in a Big D context to your organization, department, team, and the problem you are looking to solve—or the mountain you are looking to climb, for that matter.

Embrace the power of Dynamic Documentation to achieve real-world benefits. Your motivation for becoming a smarter, faster, and better employee, business owner, consultant, or organization does not really matter. It could be to solve an immediate project or problem. It could be to successfully complete your organization's five-year plan.

What does matter is simply this: your commitment to the practice of Dynamic Documentation for the long term, throughout the ranks, and across all functions. Your people need to understand that, going forward, Dynamic Documentation will be standard operating procedure and is here to stay.

They need to understand why it will benefit everyone and why their participation is critical to the entire team's success.

Then, once the bar has been set, get started! Here are seven tips for diving into Dynamic Documentation.

1. PICK A PROBLEM (OR MAYBE TWO)

Think of some specific problems you are trying to solve, or organizational "knotted shoelaces" that need attention. Everyone has a goal or situation that can be improved through better documentation practices. For example:

- If you have a project on your plate, such as a new system, regulation, or process design, use Dynamic Documentation to work through it.
- If you are looking for a promotion, there are myriad ways to use documentation to take you to the next level. Don't just try impressing your boss with what you say or your credentials—show your prowess with real deliverables.
- If you are looking to move your team to higher performance, inventory your team's documentation skills and develop a plan to patch the holes and amp up your strengths.

Most of us can't simultaneously train for the Ironman Triathlon, start a business, parent our kids, and be president of the PTA. (If you can, I'm impressed!) The same is true in our work world. Most of us are rarely successful if we take on too many projects at once. Focus your efforts. Choose one problem, maybe two, and get started.

Next, prepare to reach your goal by setting a hard deadline (e.g., "I will clean up the M-drive by November," or "I will document the new inventory system process by June 15th"). This makes your project "dynamic" (i.e., focused on action rather than documentation for documentation's sake).

2. LOOK AT WHERE YOU ARE GOING BEFORE LOOKING AT WHAT YOU HAVE

Maybe you have worked hard over the past decade to build a successful team or even department. Maybe you are a project manager or business analyst who has led a number of successful implementations. Or maybe you have built your own successful small business over the past twenty years. Whatever your situation, the chances are that you probably have a heck of a lot of documents, along with folders, drives, repositories, and other detritus. You have probably been moderately successful with your messy files in the past.

But don't channel all your (perhaps type A) energy on making these relics—your files, systems, or processes—perfect.

Rather, look at where you want to go, not at what you have. Don't obsess over your old ways of doing things. Focus your energy around driving the behaviors you want to see going forward.

Documentation is a powerful tool for change. But it can also be a big waste of time if you fail to connect with the *why*. "Getting documented" is not a good enough reason. Connect with a higher purpose.

Before you start your project, understand your reasons for doing it. Put this in writing and share it with your team. Such drivers might include:

- Improving clarity
- Reducing your company's risk, whether legal, financial, IT security, or other
- Making more money through sales, market share, ideas/innovation
- Saving money through time and cost efficiencies
- Improving intra-organizational communications

Then, take stock. What do you have? You might be tempted to jump in and start solving the problem by buying a new system, writing your policies, scrapping your processes, cleaning out your folders, overhauling your metadata, building intricate workflows, hiring fancy consultants, and so on. But stop and look at where you are and what you have first.

A documentation audit is like "closet shopping." That is, going through your closet before rushing out to buy new clothes. Chances are you have many items you forgot about that still appeal. Don't throw out everything in your quest to clear valuable closet space.

Ask yourself:

- What is my documentation philosophy? Is it supporting or hindering my problem?

- Which of the 5 Stages of Documentation best describes my organization, department, or team?
- How can we apply the 5 Super Standards to solve the problem? Which of the standards is the most relevant and which most needs improvement?

  ▷ **Re-Performance Standard:** This may mean weak technical writing skills or other areas of Step 3: Presenting; lack of Organizational Design concepts; documenters who don't really understand what they are documenting; or a failure to apply the necessary level of rigor to documentation.

  ▷ **Clarity Standard:** This may indicate a weakness in Step 3: Presenting, or be related to the "People" circle of the Documentation Triad.

  ▷ **Findability Standard:** This points to challenges with Step 5: Storing and Leveraging, or "Information" in the Documentation Triad.

  ▷ **Use Standard:** Usability often has to do with Step 4: Communicating, and is also symptomatic of all three circles in the Documentation Triad—the "Information" circle (people can't find things or it's hard to find things), the "Process" circle (there is no organizational structure or discipline for using the documents), or the "People" circle (no one is instructed, communicated, trained, enforced, or encouraged to use documentation correctly).

  ▷ **Engagement Standard:** Here, the problem may relate to Step 3: Presenting, but the issues may stem all the way from Step 1: Capturing.

- What documents or information does your team access the most? Where are they domiciled?
- Which documents would the team need if you or your team members were to win the lottery and leave the organization for greener pastures?
- What documentation is usable? What is not?

- Are the documents out of date? Have they lost their value with time?
- What are the key strengths of the documentation? What are the key weaknesses of the documentation?
- What are the processes for creating and leveraging documentation? How should they be improved?
- What are your methods for sharing documents, reports, and progress?
- What is your process for finding documentation? Where do you look?
- Which search criteria/terms would you like to see to help you retrieve your documentation?
- Do your systems and tools meet your needs? Are there newer, more robust methodologies that can or should be considered and adopted?

3. GROUP YOUR DOCUMENTS AND TACKLE THE UNDERLYING PROCESS

Next order of business: Group your documents to get a "line of sight" or a comprehensive view of what you currently have. For many problems you will be asked to solve, you will start with a blank slate. But for many others, especially in the corporate world, you will start with a daunting number of databases, file folders, processes, policies, systems, SharePoint sites, and (of course) documents.

If you are staring at thousands of documents—perhaps across repositories, systems, and departments—you are probably wondering where to go next. The good news is that no matter how many documents you have or how complex your cleanup job or problem is, these basic concepts can be used to sort your documents and give you a line of sight.

- **Work-in-progress files:** Clear the path to your work in progress. These are the files that should be at your fingertips. They should be ready to go and easily visible for your team.
- **Archives and reference files:** You wouldn't put the manual for your furnace on your home office desk. Think of the same for your archived, old, or reference files. Put them somewhere (like your

basement) where you can find them but where they aren't in your way. For things you access more regularly, like templates, training materials, and process documents, store them in a library.

- **ROT (redundant, outdated, and trivial—aka, "trash"):** Your ROT files will drag you down. Chuck them or stash them. Documents are not like junk in your garage; they don't take up much room and they don't cost much to store or to remove. You don't need to call junk removal, either. Delete ROT files or, if you are too nervous about deleting (especially if you are doing a big cleanup), put your old documents in a temporary ROT folder.

Then, tackle the underlying process. The process you are trying to fix may be obvious. Maybe you are starting a new division that needs processes or maybe you have been tasked with improving one of your company's formal functions, like accounts payable, maintenance, or project management.

Process issues can be less obvious, too. Process is also about routines, cultural norms, practices, and behaviors that your team or company does consistently and that compound over time.

- You see patterns in people's behaviors (e.g., the entire team shares the habit of never writing things down from meetings).
- You see a recurring issue (e.g., there is a high volume of IT incidents coming from one team).
- Your documentation is a mess (e.g., there isn't a process for keeping documents in order in the first place).

For simple process issues, you have a secret weapon—the 24-Hour Rule. If your sales orders are always a mess, use the 24-Hour Rule to get your team to deal with that issue. If your team has great ideas but can't get any traction, use the 24-Hour Rule to get them to record and share their notes. If you can't get a grip on your emails, use the 24-Hour Rule to manage your email processing time.

You could also be facing a far more complex or difficult process problem. Examples abound: understanding why a division is failing, reducing your department's headcount, or implementing an ERP, to name just a few possibilities. No matter how complex the problem is, strip it down to the Dynamic Documentation basics, like having a great note-taking practice, structuring your information, piecing together to solve the problem, communicating to others, storing and leveraging new and existing materials, and then leading through your work. Dynamic Documentation is fundamentally designed to improve your processes from Little d skills to Big D applications.

4. GET YOUR TEAM TO WORK SMARTER

Then, get your team to work "smarter" (without ever actually asking them). While your people may be part (even all) of your problem, they are also your solution.

Your first choice in solving your problem is to work with the team you have. This means you need to get your team to work smarter (more efficiently and effectively). Unfortunately, the worst thing you can say to your team is "work smarter," "work harder," or, even worse, "work as hard as I do." This is a challenge, especially for business owners.

The beauty of documentation is that it's de-personalized and therefore nonconfrontational. Telling your team they have a work ethic problem is offensive, but saying you want to improve documentation practices is not. Documentation is a tool for getting your people to work smarter and a barometer for how smart they work. Use it as a gauge for performance. Don't blame the individual, and instead use documentation to move the needle.

If you are worried that your project team is behind on their project, review their files and check in on what's going on. If your technical writer or auditor isn't giving you the high-quality documentation you need, ask them to meet the Re-Performance Standard. You can measure their performance faster from opening their documents than from update meetings, during which progress can be easily fudged or embellished.

Working smarter comes with building your team's Little d documentation mindset. Your team might not realize it's a Little d documentation problem that is leading to Big D problems like lost sales, poor momentum, and slow projects. Not everyone makes the connection. The good news is that mindset is malleable in most (though not all) people. Like a computer, we can program our minds to function as we want them to. Many of us have some reprogramming to do.

Training in the latest new framework, tool, or technology won't determine your team's success or their ability to solve your immediate or future problems. But building foundational skills will. Documentation is a "back-to-basics" skill stack (such as sales, communications, presentation, managing, organization, and emotional intelligence) that transcends all trends. Though documentation will change with the times, the skill stack itself is timeless.

Then, screen for documentation skills. Your solution to your problem or your project will fail if you don't screen for the right Little d skills when hiring or promoting. I have seen business analysts who don't write anything down, senior auditors who are too good to test transactions, and technical writers who believe sounding professional means making documentation dry. I have seen leaders shake their heads at why their perfect hires with years of experience have no documentation skills.

Why do we keep making the same mistakes? Because we rarely screen for documentation skills, or more specifically those Little d skills. Big D experiences like "implemented transformation initiative" may be on your candidates' resumes, but when it comes to Little d skills like competent note-taking, organizational mindsets, follow-up ability, and personal workflow, you will have to dig to find the best person.

Documentation skills are not like "breathing" skills. Breathing is involuntary. Most people are not good at documenting—at least, not at first.

Many, if not most, managers (especially HR managers and recruiters) are not good at screening for Little d documentation skills. So, companies often get the buzzword-flinging candidate they thought they were looking for.

Documentation is hard work. Look for the person with a willingness to perform and an understanding of the importance of the unfun, unsexy, unglamorous work, and put them above the candidate talking about his business case skills from his MBA. Be upfront about the documentation work—and other "grunt work," as I call it—that you need. Too many job positions or interviewees overly glamorize what the job is about; they focus on the sexier side of the work, even if it represents only 1 percent of the job.

I have learned from my mistakes. I have underplayed the grunt work in interviews and have regretted this later, finding out that my "star" consultant felt too good to complete spreadsheets, take notes, or test invoices. Benefit from my experience and don't hide documentation or other grunt work when you are hiring. Doing so too often results in a new hire who becomes quickly disgruntled or disengaged, or ends up leaving.

I hire many people who do compliance testing, which (as you may have guessed) is not exactly sexy stuff. If a candidate tells me they enjoy and are good at testing, my experience is that they are generally right. If they don't enjoy this type of work (whether they tell me honestly or not), the candidate gets a bit squeamish. Your gut will lead you to the best person for the job. But you must be forthright about the nature of the position.

As long as I'm on the topic, let me posit that grunt work, like documentation, is not "difficult" work, per se. And yet it isn't necessarily "brainless" work, either. It's actually a form of smart work. I'm not saying Jeff Bezos is worth over $100 billion today because he did tasks like data entry *really* well. But I am saying one of the key things that separated him from other smart guys was his ability to push through grunt work (e.g., raising money from friends and family, yelling at developers, negotiating with book publishers, working long hours, packing books on his knees before Amazon's first delivery).

You're looking for that special person with real fire in their belly. Little d documentation skills are greatly needed even though few people like them and even fewer are good at them. Screen for these skills carefully.

5. DON'T FORGET YOUR OWN LEARNING

Don't forget your own learning. There is a universal need for Little d documentation skills. Documentation frees you to improve and expand your work, whether you are in the trenches, are running your own company, or are the CEO of a multinational.

Excellence in any endeavor requires repetition, and Dynamic Documentation is no different. The more you see and the wider the variety of work you dive into, the greater your career progress will be. Read, research, and talk to as many people as you can about the subject to continually improve your breadth and depth of understanding. Courses are OK. But don't be a course junkie your whole life unless you really enjoy them. Apply the information you've gained to real-world challenges.

Between work and little kiddos, I don't have much time for courses. I don't have any time for conferences. And while I do read a few books a month, I don't read as much as I'd like to. The way I expand my documentation skills is through *work*. I need to make money while I am learning, and that is the reality of my situation. I stick my hand up and say yes to every assignment that comes my way, even when the undertaking is way outside my comfort zone. I take on the most challenging assignments and rely on Dynamic Documentation to succeed.

If you don't have the variety or immediate exposure to client work in your current job, get it from reading and courses. The 6 Steps of Dynamic Documentation are there for you. Little d opportunities are abundant. So, learn under fire (while you are making money, even if the pay isn't superb) wherever you can.

Dynamic Documentation is about training for bursts of high-speed activity. Think of yourself as a disciplined, highly trained athlete. Documentation demands laser-focused brain power, not passive meeting attendance, answering trivial emails, or looking busy.

Have you ever used interval training at your health club? Dynamic Documentation is like CrossFit for your work. Dynamic Documentation is about high-intensity work interspersed with periods of rest and relief. Do the "sprinting" to get your plan, report, analysis, spreadsheet, or proposal to a "good enough" state. Then put it away for a few days and work on something else, or give yourself the weekend to rest on it. Your brain will work on your document *in the background* (like a processor) while you aren't looking or thinking about it. This is the miracle of the documentation sprint. Work smart (and hard), and then take a break.

Work hard on the problem at hand. Push it, pull it, or (if you have to) drag it across the finish line. Remember: You're an athlete. A documentation athlete. Dig in. Push!

And as you do, remember not to let the quest for perfect be the enemy of good. That means you don't need to customize every feature of the new system and, no, you don't need to make every document look pretty enough to hang in the Louvre. The proverbial 80/20 rule (where 80 percent of results come from 20 percent of efforts) makes a lot of sense.

6. STOP TO SMELL THE ROSES

If you are close to the finish line, but find yourself on a meandering path or extra lap, stop. Take a mental breather. Maybe you are faced with unending rounds of edits. Or too many people weighing in on your templates. Or your management is stuck in a fog of indecisiveness. End the race if you can.

Most work problems or projects are never closed forever, nor should they be. Documents, documentation systems, and processes are about driving the future—a future that is always changing. Get your solution to the point of "good enough" and keep it open to iteration, feedback, communication, and continuous improvement. Bake lean documentation into your follow-up process.

Next, move on to bigger and bolder challenges. This is about much more than just increasing money or climbing the corporate ladder—this is what you were destined to do. What you have been *training* to do. Work, like life, is just a series of problems in search of solutions. The nice thing about work is that we are paid for it.

With your Dynamic Documentation practice in hand, take on whatever problem the company, team, department, or industry throws at you.

7. REVIEW THE DYNAMIC DOCUMENTATION CHEAT SHEET

Finally, use this Dynamic Documentation Cheat Sheet for maximum immediate impact on your work and the problem you are solving, and any new problems, too. You have my guarantee.

Dynamic Documentation Cheat Sheet

▶ **"Get" documentation.** Smarter organizations don't just "do" documentation, they "get" it. Your company or team needs the right philosophy for understanding how to turn documentation into its superpower.

▶ **Don't forget Little d.** Recognize the Big D projects on your plate. Build a foundation of Little d skills and disciplines to make your Big D projects—and your everyday work—wildly successful.

▶ **Identify which of the 5 Stages of Documentation you are in.** Stage 1 (no documentation), Stage 2 (documentation "lite"), Stage 3 (OK but suboptimal), Stage 4 (optimized documentation), or Stage 5 (overdocumentation).

PRACTICE THE "SECRETS" OF DYNAMIC DOCUMENTATION:

1 **The Skill Stack Solution,** which tells us to identify the specific documentation skills for each project or task and to identify our own skills and those of our team—and to build and source additional skills as necessary.

2 **The Next-Action Interview,** which recommends that, whenever you are stuck on a problem, think about interviewing someone to get the information, insight, and inspiration you need to get to the next step.

3 **The 24-Hour Rule,** which states that you *must* rethink, reprocess, or rewrite information within 24 hours of hearing it. (Or in simpler terms: just do *something* with the information.)

4 **Use What You Know Draft,** which means that you build your first drafts of documents based on what you know using the information you have and your experiences and instincts.

5 **"What's Working and What's Not Working" Memo,** which means reporting out at a point in time to voice your opinion about the project and to determine next steps.

6 **Action-Over-Perfection Protocol,** which reminds us that documents and documentation systems that drive momentum are more valuable than "perfection." Documentation systems and practices should be designed around driving action and changing outcomes, not around perfect files, metadata, or configuration.

7 **The Groundhog Trap,** which directs us to use documentation techniques to stop (trap) runaround conversations about future projects or past decisions.

Apply the 6 Steps of Dynamic Documentation to work smarter, faster, and better. Step 1: Capturing, Step 2: Structuring, Step 3: Presenting, Step 4: Communicating, Step 5: Storing and Leveraging, and Step 6: Leading and Innovating. (Remember, the steps won't always work in order and sometimes you will need certain steps and not others.)

If you need to remember it, document it. Your short-term memory will let you down. So, jot down your meeting notes, log your to-dos, or send that email now to capture information and avoid losing it for good.

Write more. The more you write, the better you will get at it. This will make you a better documenter *and* a better writer. Grab opportunities to write where you can.

Write fast. Write fast to accelerate your focus and give your work a "hard push." In today's distracted world, this is an invaluable skill.

Build, fill in, revise—and rinse, repeat. Think "lean." Lean and dynamic go hand in hand. Lean means biting off what you can chew, doing it quickly, getting to "good enough," and building iteratively.

Template your work. Find a few templates to help you to scale and standardize your work and your life. (But stay away from Template Hell.)

Use curb appeal to "sell" your documentation. A document needs to hold its reader's attention, no matter what it's about. Make your documents engaging—even fun—where you can.

Share your documentation and put it into action. Communication is a two-way street. You get value from documentation when you learn how to share it.

Use documentation as a subtle, but powerful, form of influence. Documentation makes you a leader in your own right.

Don't assume your team knows how to document. No one is born knowing how to document. You need to hire, fire, and train your team for documentation skills.

Don't be a documentation dork. Don't obsess over documenting every meeting, recording everything you need to do, or detailing everything you eat. Documentation is a means to a greater end.

Release your super brain. Your documentation system releases your super brain. Not needing to remember that meeting, your to-do list, how you came to that decision, how a process works, or where you kept that file—it's one less thing to stress about when you know your documentation has your back. Let documentation practices be your loyal helper, letting your super brain shine.

CHAPTER 10

—

Applying Dynamic Documentation at Home

Getting smarter works at home, too.

D ynamic Documentation is about improving your work *and* your life. The career and business points—such as greater clarity, introspection, organization, and movement—will improve your personal and family life, too.

It may seem like a stretch to talk about corporate documentation (such as legal records, project plans, board minutes, and large enterprise content management systems) on the same plane as your personal to-do list, but they truly *are* on the same plane. Here's the commonality: They are all about capturing information to drive action for the future. The more you can see the two dimensions of documentation as connected, the more successful you will be in both worlds.

Right now, we are talking about *little* Little d—we are focused on you.

MANAGING THE INFORMATION IN OUR LIVES

When I talk about personal documentation, I am talking about developing a deeper connection with documentation as a tool for making changes to your life. This is not feel-good self-help. Documentation is a follow-up tool. It is an enforcer. It is comfort for you when you need to think.

We have a strong relationship with the information we bring into our day. Whether it is picking up items at the grocery store, thinking through a complex engineering problem, or dealing with a problem with our teenager, our processes of managing information control our days and ultimately our lives.

In today's workplace, we've come to recognize that the lives of employees don't exist in neat silos anymore. The old days are gone. Gone for good. The advances of technology mean work follows us home, and home follows us to work. Many of us are always on call in business, but also as parents, spouses, friends, Little League coaches, or whatever other hats we wear in our lives. Modern businesses realize their employees have lives outside work and that an employee with a healthy work-life balance is likely to be a happier, healthier, and smarter employee. The fact is, our business lives and our home lives are no longer separated in the ways they once were—one bleeds into the other, and there's no going back from that.

Although your personal, home, and work lives may not be exactly how you want them all the time—and they will tug and pull at each other in opposite directions—they are deeply connected. They should work in harmony, however imperfectly.

Use the power of Dynamic Documentation to move beyond your company and make your whole life successful. I urge you to see opportunities to use Dynamic Documentation to improve your work, career, personal life, and home life, too.

A Tool for Your Personal Life

By personal life, I am talking about taking care of yourself—your mental and physical health and your development. This also addresses your relationships, your friendships, your hobbies, your interests, and your involvement in the community.

Documentation is cheaper and often more effective than a coach, trainer, or therapist. But even coaches, trainers, and therapists will use documentation techniques to help you to get on the right path.

A Tool for Family Management

Home or family management is all about "managing" your spouse or significant other, kids, parents, pets, close friends, relatives, roommates, or whoever is in your tight circle. Related activities include managing your schedules, assets, and finances, all while keeping people fed and healthy and making sure the school slips are in on time.

Given the number of dependent humans, itineraries, must-do events, differing vacation dates, and so on, your home life can seem unmanageable in comparison to your work life. That is why home management requires systems and strategies to support your most important goals for yourself and your loved ones.

When it comes to your home life, here are the types of tasks that require these systems and strategies to keep them running smoothly:

- Cleaning
- Tidying and organizing
- Laundry
- Childcare
- Kids' activities
- Pet management
- Household bill management
- Vacation planning
- Family appointments (dentist, doctor, therapist, teacher interviews)
- House supply management
- Garbage management (yes, this is a thing in my house, especially with local green initiatives)
- House paperwork

- Family events, birthdays
- Taxes
- Vehicle management
- Family calendar
- Insurance
- Savings and investments

As someone with three kids (eight and under), two older stepkids, a dog, a dragon (it's a lizard in the basement), and (let me not forget) a husband, I get just how hard home management is. It makes work feel like an all-inclusive trip to Cancún. Home management is a massive coordination effort and, for some people like me, harder than work or even personal documentation for a few reasons:

- Most of us do not have a lot of support resources when it comes to managing the house, unlike at the office. (Unless you are Elon Musk, whom I have heard has a "nanny manager.")
- Most of us don't have a lot of formality in managing our personal lives and our homes, so the management is typically haphazard at best.
- It is harder to get family members to do what we want than our subordinates or coworkers, who are "forced" into it through the context of work. (Unfortunately, my kids see themselves as superiors, not subordinates.)
- There is almost no training out there on home management, except for whatever your parents may have taught you. (Many of us, like me, ignored our parents anyway.) We tend to learn it on the fly.
- You can be the CEO of a Fortune 500 company and still get yelled at when at home to pick up your dirty socks. At work, people may do what you tell them to do. But in your family life, you need compelled collaboration to get others to agree.
- You can pick your team members (who come with their own documentation styles) if you run a business or manage a team at work, but you don't have as much choice at home.

It took me years to clue in to using Dynamic Documentation practices to manage my personal and home life with the diligence it needed. But please save yourself the agony, and use the practices in your personal world as well.

DOCUMENTATION AND THE CARE AND FEEDING OF *YOU*

Let's talk about mental health. COVID-19, working from home, kids screaming while you work, the onslaught of news and social media, doomscrolling, phones buzzing, threats of economic meltdown—these have all added to our mental health pressures in recent years. It's an avalanche of noise, all day, every day.

In the olden days, when humans toiled in the field or in the factory, we taxed our bodies. Today, with the rise of the service sector, we tax our minds. Unfortunately, we aren't taxing our minds with deep, focused, hard-thinking work either. We are taxing our minds with too much beeping, too much media, too many useless meetings, and too many to-dos. We are overloaded with meetings and busywork, so we can't get our real work done.

Adult life is taxing. Mental health is a huge topic today, and for good reasons. No one has the answer for perfect mental health. I certainly don't have any answers for serious mental health issues. But I do have an answer for improving your mental fitness: documentation.

Possibly one of the biggest, and most under-acknowledged, benefits of any type of documentation is its positive impact on mental health. Documentation relieves stress. Documentation is a tool for fighting the enemy of distraction and for taking control of your life. It allows for self-reflection and for gaining greater clarity and insight into your life. Use documentation to protect your mind.

Use a To-Do List for Distraction and Anxiety

In his 2005 *Harvard Business Review* article "Overloaded Circuits," Edward M. Hallowell coined the term "attention deficit trait (ADT)." Unlike attention-deficit/hyperactivity disorder (ADHD), which has a genetic component, ADT is caused by the environment and your reaction to it. ADT means brain over-load, causing a state of distractibility, panic, and impatience. ADT affects even the most competent and successful people, including executives. Maybe you have experienced this? If you have experienced ADT, it is as if you are running around like the proverbial chicken with its head cut off. I have been there. It is not a fun way to be.

Sleep, exercise, and good food will help you to prevent and alleviate ADT (just as they do for many other mental and physical health issues). But that isn't the only way it can be prevented. Documentation is an underrated way of helping you with ADT, too, whether the issues are minor cases of distract-ibility or more serious issues of not being able to move any projects or initia-tives in your life forward.

Stress comes from having too much in your head. Documentation is a way of getting this information out of your head and controlling your stress levels. Documenting what you want to get done is one of the smartest ways to man-age your stress. It gives you control over your day and satisfaction that you are moving forward. Both are necessary for feeling good about your day. Between our work and personal lives, we can have so many to-dos that they can cause us to blow a mental fuse. Take control of your to-dos, or they will control you.

Take Control of Bad Days

When you're having a bad day, documenting a few simple things and cross-ing them off your list will make you feel better. There's something therapeu-tic in crossing things off. It doesn't work every time, but it's worth a try.

One of the problems with bad days is we often get (way) less done, which ends up making our day even worse. Sometimes it's a setback in our business. Sometimes it's a family thing, or no sleep from kids being up all night or suf-fering a cold. We all have our bad days, some worse than others. Bingeing Netflix and eating Doritos rarely gets you feeling better. But simple documen-tation techniques can help you, even just a bit, to get through your bad day.

If you are having a bad day, take your pen or your note-taking app and write yourself a few *super* easy but beneficial things to do. "Make bed," "Drink water," "Clean desk," "Call Mom." Cross them off as you get through them.

Our stress and our ability to execute are tightly connected. The more we get done, the better we feel. It's hard to feel your best when you aren't getting anything done. Even if you are having a bad day, you'll feel better if you write something down and get it done. By tracking your to-dos, you may also find that you've been accomplishing a lot more than you realized, which gives you good perspective for those times when you can't remember if you got anything at all done last week. Turns out you did! Go, you!

Journal to Give Yourself Perspective

Journaling has been popularized by the self-help movement, by Oprah, and by so many other gurus. You could really say journaling has made a comeback. Throughout history, there have been many brilliant people who have used journals to shape their thoughts and their lives—Napoleon, Oscar Wilde, Anne Frank, and Abraham Lincoln, to name a few. Their journals have been accessible posthumously for us to understand their worlds and, in turn, learn about the history and struggles of their lives and times.

The practices of journaling and to-do list management are blurring today in modern definitions and use. Like the to-do list, journaling is essentially writing for yourself (not for others) that helps you to control your day. While to-do list management is focused on what you need to do, journaling is more focused on what you have done or acts as reflection and processing of your current events and life. Recording your thoughts helps to gain insight into your behaviors and moods and think through better decisions or solutions for your life. Experts claim journaling does wonders for your health.

Clear Your Head of Problems, Overthinking, and Obsessing

Do you have a friend who seems to have everything, but you find her stressing over her living room furniture or her Starbucks order? Or another friend who stresses over his tee time and frequent flyer miles?

While these "stresses" may annoy you, this is not entirely your friends' faults. Our brains are designed for problem-solving. We are constantly scanning our environment for problems, and even our Starbucks order can be a problem if our brain can't find another problem to work on. Our minds spin on problems, trying to solve them until they reach some form of resolution. That is what your mind is designed to do. It's just doing its job.

People go to therapy to take their problems out of their brains and release them through their voices into the air. Therapy is a form of problem-solving. Documentation is another, much cheaper form of therapeutic problem-solving where you release the problem onto paper.

Keeping too many problems, such as analyses, decisions, or notes in your head will exhaust your brain. Your brain is wrapped up in the work, home, or personal problem and can't let it go. This is a selfish reason I have for committing so many notes, ideas, concepts, and analyses for my clients onto paper. It stresses me to hold them in my head.

Let Go of the Past

Why hold on to the one bad performance report you received five years ago? Why hold on to a nasty email from a former client? Why keep emails from an ex?

Dealing with the information clutter in your life is not always easy. Information clutter, like the physical clutter around us, takes a toll on us. Clearing information clutter can be as cathartic as purging our physical spaces and tossing out old junk.

Like cleaning out your garage, let this information go and be gone forever. You should ask yourself these questions before hanging on to information:

- Will it help someone?
- Will it serve a genuine purpose and be useful?
- Do you *have* to keep this for legal or reference reasons (e.g., taxes, medical files)?
- Does it spark interest or make you feel good?
- Is it something you want to share?
- Will it make you more money?

If your answer each of these questions is no, toss it. Throw out that old rejection letter. Delete those ten thousand old emails from five years ago. Go through your filing cabinets and shred old documents you don't actually need. Do you still need to hang onto the take-out menu from the pizza place that shut down three years ago? Probably not.

Deal with Loose Ends

Lack of closure, especially as it relates to information, takes a psychic toll on us.

- Your incomplete to-do lists
- Client deliverables or files you never handed over
- Loose ends from a project you "almost" finished
- Meeting notes not recorded or circulated
- Courses you didn't finish
- Feedback you were supposed to give
- Prospects you never followed up with

What else would you add to this list? Develop a strategy for loose ends. Don't let them overwhelm your mental well-being.

I will admit that I go through phases of expansion and phases of cleanup in my life. Expansion means I want to do new things—work with new clients, start new projects, engage in new activities, attend new events. Cleanup means I want to clear the backlog. (Top business thinker Dorie Clark calls these modes "heads up" and "heads down.")

When I think to myself, "OMG, I am bouncing from task to task, I have too many things piling up, and I can't get to the tasks I keep meaning to do each day," then I need a cleanup period. This may be an afternoon, a week, or it can be a month or even two months. It is my mental health that tells me I need to put the brakes on. This is when I take a list of everything bothering me (e.g., client files, administration, my daughter's piano practicing, a messy office, unfinished projects) and I do a hard all-hands-on-deck push to get the things done.

After an all-hands-on-deck push to clear this list, I have energy again to move to an expansion phase.

Most of us are expanding and cleaning up daily in a type of circadian rhythm. You may think of this phenomenon as simply the ongoing tugs and pulls on your life. Truth be told, you need cleanup to make expansion work. Most of us can't take on twenty projects—or five volunteer boards, three team sports, a home renovation, and three kids, for that matter—and still be a valuable team player. Using cleanup modes, whether they are daily, weekly, or monthly, forces us to be realistic in what we take on and useful to our teammates, family, and community.

Add Structure in an Unstructured World

In our parents' day, they went to work, dealt with work at the office, and left it there when they came home. Now we are dealing with work at home and with home at work. Technology has removed the boundaries between work and home and between clients.

The trend of working from home (or WFM) sounds nice in theory, but it is just increasing our number of choices of things to focus on, which leads to distraction, task-switching, paralysis, and stress. Technology has taken down our boundaries, which means you need to put up your own.

The increase in choices is a distraction in itself. If you are sitting at work, perhaps it's in a virtual office, on Tuesday at 10:35 AM, these are some things that might be calling for your attention:

- Should I read this email from my kid's school? Jeez, I missed the last bake sale.
- I really need to get this memo out to the boss by the end of the day.
- I should check how my investment account is doing today.
- It's Allison's birthday! I need to write her a Facebook message.
- If I don't write down these notes from today's meeting, I am sure to forget them.
- There's an awesome online sale at Pottery Barn today.
- I really want to jump on this new project.
- Oh man, I have to tie off loose ends from my old project.
- I should really follow up on that request I submitted to IT.
- Do we need milk?

There is a lot of talk of the modern workforce being "knowledge workers" nowadays. But this is an elusive term. Everyone has knowledge, from CEOs to plumbers to pastry chefs. And really, knowledge on its own doesn't make an employee or consultant valuable. (You can know *how* to make a pastry, but it's actually making it that matters.)

What we really should be talking about are deliverables or time workers. Companies today need people who can manage deliverables and time. Your ability to manage deliverables and time comes first from managing your daily choices and from chunking out your time. Documentation helps you make these choices more deliberate.

DYNAMIC DOCUMENTATION AT HOME

Now, let's take your life to new levels of efficiency, productivity, and fulfillment outside of the workplace. Bring the 6 Steps of Dynamic Documentation home.

Step 1. Capturing: Managing Your To-Dos

To-do lists are the foundation of personal and family documentation that kick off and drive all other activities. A to-do list transcends and fuses our personal, home, and work lives. To-do lists function in harmony with Dynamic Documentation.

They are the perfect example of Step 1: Capturing (e.g., to-dos, ideas, things to buy, errands, goals), although technically they span multiple steps. You Capture, Structure, Present, Communicate, and Store and Maintain (and then Lead and Innovate through osmosis) what's on your to-do list.

We might think of to-do lists as just something that needs to be done that day. But they are really about ongoing tasks and personal projects, which is where the complexity lies. "Project" means any series of tasks to accomplish a goal, including training for a marathon, writing a book, renovating your basement, planning a vacation, and so on.

There are a lot of great to-do list tips and tricks out there. I have distilled my favorites below, garnered from the experts.

David Allen's Getting Things Done

David Allen is the guru of to-do list management. Allen advocates creating lists of all areas of your life to get the "inventory" of all your tasks. At first, I found this too daunting, but the more I get into it, the more I realize this method works.

Allen helps solve the problem with traditional to-do lists that we don't get to everything on our lists each day. He teaches you to accept this as part of life. Our days are dynamic. Your boss comes into your office with an urgent request. Your kid gets sick. A potential client calls with a huge new opportunity. Your friend gives you tickets to the hockey game.

The Getting Things Done method (GTD) is about creating to-do lists and being adaptable, or flexible. He doesn't advocate sticking religiously to detailed plans each day. He teaches you to keep running to lists where you deal with tasks through a mix of the context, time, and energy available for them. If you have ten minutes between meetings, you can call to book a haircut, but you wouldn't call a client for a discussion you know could go on for a long time.

I struggled initially with how Allen doesn't talk about priorities. He believes anything that has your attention should be captured and dealt with in some manner, no matter whether it is a "big thing" (e.g., buying a house, getting a new job) or a "little thing" (e.g., buying a can opener, taking the dog for a walk).

The more I matured, the more I realized that the GTD focus on the little things is brilliant. The little things in life—like taking out the garbage, getting an oil change, and making sure your kids brush their teeth—are essential to the functioning of our lives and are even satisfying in many ways. The truth is that they do have our attention, whether we track them well or not. (Remember, your brain is looking to solve problems, whether you are fighting a bear or fighting for your Starbucks order.)

Also, the big things and little things in your life collide when we don't expect them to. Getting your oil changed may seem less important than calling back the president of your top client. But if your car breaks down on your way to meet your top client because you didn't get your oil changed, then this will alter your concept of priority.

GTD relates to Dynamic Documentation because it has a huge focus on capturing, structuring, planning, doing, and clearing your mental space.

Andy Frisella's The Power List

The "Power List" is another approach to managing the to-do list challenge. I particularly like the insights of entrepreneur and speaker Andy Frisella, whom I heard speak at a conference. This approach suggests putting "5 critical tasks" on your to-do list that you need to get done each day to advance your life. This is your Power List.

Now, here is the catch. The things you put on this list need to be things you have to *stretch* yourself to do. They cannot be things that are in your routine, or things you "feel" like doing.

- If you have fallen off the wagon when it comes to the gym and you need to push yourself to go, then put this on the list for that day.
- If you have to nudge yourself to make that important sales call, then do it.
- If you have procrastinated on a certain piece of work for a few days now (maybe weeks), do it.
- If you need to have a difficult conversation with someone who works for you, put it on the list.

On the flip side, if you have a great eating or fitness routine, don't put it on the list. You focus only on areas where you really need to give yourself momentum, motivation, or a kick in the behind.

Unlike *Getting Things Done*, this method is priorities-based. It forces you to think about what is most important for you that day for moving your life forward. It is also a process that makes you think about what systems in your life are working or not one day at a time.

The Power List concept is like Dynamic Documentation in that it has a strong focus on discernment—that is, deciding what truly matters to you.

Sacred Buckets

The Sacred Buckets method is about managing your day by sacred areas (or "buckets," as I say) of your life. This is one that most of us do naturally but not formally.

While I have heard a similar concept from gurus like Tony Robbins and Dr. Phil before, Karma Brown in her bestseller *The 4% Fix* crystallizes the concept beautifully. She talks about a "Focused Four," which are her areas for generating her daily to-dos. Her personal key "buckets" are Health/Wellness, Creativity, Family, and Productivity. She attacks her to-do list by picking from each bucket each day.

Your buckets are sections of your life that you have defined as what matters to you most. They may be:

- Spouse, partner, dating
- Kids, grandkids, nieces and nephews
- Health, fitness, well-being, spirituality
- Career
- Client work
- Managing people who work for you
- Prospecting, marketing, and sales
- Hobbies, teams, sports
- Writing and blogging
- Reading, research, learning
- Education, coursework

We all have different buckets depending on what's on our plate, what we do, what our goals are, and what stage of life we're in. You may have four buckets, or you might have three or two or maybe six. You can swap buckets in and out depending on what matters and what is going on throughout the year. You can make your buckets whatever size you want, too.

As I write this, my buckets are: Family, Client Work (what's on my plate), Sales/Growth (how to grow), Writing/Reading/Learning, and Health/Wellness. These buckets have changed over the years. I used to have a Volunteering bucket, a Friends/Social Life bucket, and a Hobbies bucket—but the work and family buckets have pushed them over for now.

The beauty of buckets is that they are intentional. No matter how busy you are, you still control how you define your buckets. They give context to your life, your problems, and your objectives. They are also tactical. They help you take your ethereal goals (like New Year's resolutions) and pull them into everyday planning. I wanted to write this book for years, but I could never find time to do it. Once I created a Writing bucket, I was able to "eat the elephant," as they say, by chewing off little bits of the book project every day.

Sacred Buckets give your day balance and save you from dropping the balls in your life. If you are doing something in your key buckets each day, you are less likely to let your relationships, kids, business, side gig, sales, customers, staff, or volunteer work slide. For most of us, there is always more you could be doing for your job, clients, or career. Or maybe you have never-ending family issues. If that is you, the Sacred Buckets method is perfect for giving all parts of your life attention, not just the squeakiest project, client, or family member.

The Sacred Buckets method is like Dynamic Documentation in that it helps with structuring your to-dos and your day. It brings lean thinking into your life by accepting "good enough" in how you handle your demanding boss, your biggest project, your house, your Parents' Association group, your meals, or your birthday planning.

Which capture method do I use or recommend?

All of them. I use a Frankensteinian, stitched-together combination of all of these to-do list methods. I am a huge GTD fan and use it as my foundation. But the Power List is wonderful to nudge me into doing what I should be doing that day and not what I feel like doing (although I *never* get to all five stretch goals). I use the Sacred Buckets method conceptually to bring balance to my life and structure to goal planning. Trial what works best for you. You will probably find some combination that works, too.

Step 2. Structuring: Controlling Your Day-To-Day

In your personal world and home management, structure is about putting all your to-dos, errands, family needs, or house projects in a structure where they actually get done and don't just get talked about. It is about systems and processes for keeping your to-dos running semiautomatically.

Calendar, daily actions, and immediate actions

Once you get your to-do items on paper, move or structure them into how they will be actioned by:

- Moving some into your calendar to be done at specific times
- Moving some onto your next-action list
- Moving it into your spouse's, kid's, nanny's, or someone else in your family sphere's to-do list
- Moving some onto a "someday/maybe projects" list
- Moving some onto project lists

Even if you aren't paid to do it, there is sometimes a much higher cost of error in your personal world of missed to-dos. To name a personal few: missed Mother's Day Tea, forgotten soccer sign-ups (three years in a row), and botched vacation planning.

Dividing tasks and going wide and deep

David Allen talks about thinking of your life on horizontal and vertical axes—which I think of as "going wide" and "going deep." You need to be constantly scanning across ("going wide") your life to make sure you aren't dropping any balls (e.g., appointments, calls, workouts, homework, administration, scheduling). You also need focus ("going deep") on areas of your life that need it (e.g., your work, a book you're writing, a problem your kid is having, a business you're launching).

This is another one of David Allen's brilliant concepts. But I think you can take it one step further. Most people lean to one side or the other—they either prefer doing wide tasks or deep tasks. This may dictate the type of career they go into (e.g., if you love going wide, you might go into sales, but if you love going deep, you may be better suited for writing, academic work, or computer programming). I believe you should apply this concept to how you work in your family or personal relations as a "team."

In our house, I am a deep person. I don't like running around or being interrupted. (Not saying I don't do it, but it just isn't my preference.) This makes me best suited for deliverables-based client work, writing proposals, writing assignments, client reports, and (you guessed it) documentation.

My husband is a wide person. He loves small, short tasks—emails, phone calls, working angles, driving around. You get the picture. This makes him better suited to household errands (he *loves* errands), sales for our business, and family administration. If my kids' school calls, they never reach me (because I'm on airplane mode). But they reach my hubby.

Systems and processes

Structure in your personal and family world is also about your systems and processes. This is similar to Organizational Design, except applied to you, your family, and people in your personal sphere.

- **Meal planning:** My husband and I used to plan meals on the fly. It was a disaster. We would end up with either hungry kids and nothing to feed them, weeks of greasy take-out, or throwing out about $400 a week on Costco overbuys (which I wish was an exaggeration). Despite our best intentions, we never feel like putting any thinking into cooking (at least at this stage of our lives). The conclusion from this is that we resorted to meal-prep services—we outsourced most of the management of our meals. (Note that this isn't for you if you *are* a good meal planner. Some nights we spend over $50 on a home-made pasta dish kit.)

- **Diet:** I am by no means a diet expert. But I do know that most diets don't work because of a failure of the system. Or more specifically, a failure of the system to meet the needs of the individual. I have a friend who stopped eating sugar (completely), feels great, and has stuck to this diet for years. When I attempt no-sugar, no-bread, no-gluten, no-dairy, or no-something diets, all I can think about is sugar, bread, gluten, dairy, or whatever something else I am missing. Intermittent fasting (where you eat in an eight-hour window) is the only "system" that has worked for me. But again, this system doesn't work for everyone's body.

- **Exercise:** In my twenties, I would drive across the city and wait in line for the best workout class I could find. This was a bad system compounded by having too much time on my hands. I now do fifteen minutes a day (I know, not a model fitness routine) at home on the Peloton. I am not in the greatest shape of my life, but it's a "better-than-nothing" system that works for now.

- **Babysitting:** A great babysitting schedule is a lifesaver for our family. We have a wonderful sitter who is practically a family member and comes three evenings a week. We don't have three date nights a week, either (if you were wondering). We usually use this time for working, errands, taking the kids to activities, or recovering a bit.

Step 3. Presenting: Visualizing Your Success

Presenting for your personal and family world isn't about fancy graphics or anything cool-looking. It is about using visual cues to guide and motivate you. Often, it's the most rudimentary cues that work best.

- **To-do list visuals:** When it comes to visualizing your to-dos, what makes you tick? Tying a string around your finger, sticky notes on your computer, your whiteboard, your family calendar, or your fancy app? While I keep a running electronic (I call it "Getting Things Done") list, this isn't enough to keep me focused task to task. I keep a piece of paper next to me where I scribble and scream notes ("Remember to respond to Luke!" and "Call the dentist!!!") to keep me going.

- **Calendars:** My mother-in-law loves our big, old-fashioned family calendar. It is in my kitchen, but I walk by it and never look at it. This visual cue just doesn't work for me. But I do use Outlook reminders extensively.

- **Vision boards and other motivational tricks:** Vision boards are a documentation exercise popularized by Rhonda Byrne's 2006 film and book, *The Secret.* This is where you actually create a collage of where you want to go or goals you want to achieve, like your dream house, car, and physique. Many experts believe in this, too, although your documentation may be less flashy than pictures of models and mansions. Maybe this is the consultant in me, but once a year, I do my goals in a PowerPoint! (I know it's corny, but it helps to visualize bullets and make plans like I would for a client.)

Step 4. Communicating: Connecting with Family . . . and Your Social Network

Like your work world, the biggest source of conflict in your home life is often poor communication. Good communication makes your home life smoother.

You need to communicate with everyone running, living in, or involved in your house or immediate circles. Communications apply to your broader personal circles, such as your friends, coaches, trainers, or running buddy, to amp up your accountability.

Personal accountability

When I think of documentation that I do for myself, I think of stuff like my to-do lists, project lists, and journaling. I imagine them as just for me. But if you have worked with coaches, personal trainers, or therapists, they will probably ask you to document things like your goals, your eating, and your emotions. Sharing these personal diaries with hired professionals or even close friends and confidants can be powerful.

If you are forced to write down everything you eat and drink and every exercise you do for your personal trainer, you are more likely to see noticeable improvements in those areas. I have done this, and trust me, it works better than any miracle pill. Having to "hand in" tracking sheets to your trainer increases your success rate dramatically (through a bit of guilt and "coming to Jesus," at least in my case).

Home meetings or scheduling

I have heard many self-help experts talk about a weekly meeting with your family. This doesn't work for my family, but we do use a "weekly schedule." I email a weekly schedule to my husband every Sunday with what's going on, who is doing what, errands, who needs to be home, who needs to pick the kids up, and other fun stuff.

My husband used to be particularly bad, telling me at the last minute, "Oh sorry, I have to go for drinks with Dave," at 5:30, usually 2 minutes before he needed me to leave to get the kids. The weekly schedule has helped us with being proactive and minimizing surprises.

Social media

Before social media, you could say there wasn't much of a "communicating" step when it came to personal documentation. But social media has changed this forever.

No longer are our personal thoughts locked in our journals by our bedside. Many people process their thoughts through social media and look to their friends or "fans" to communicate their lives and seek validation through the process.

Tech entrepreneur, investor, and podcaster Naval Ravikant uses Twitter as a form of "journaling" (with over 1.8 million people reading). I once had a friend who posted on Facebook her step-by-step weight-loss plan, including pictures of what she ate that day, her workouts, and her progress. Do you think she was successful? Darn right! She was using communication as a powerful force for accountability. I am too chicken to do this, but I could have saved a bit of money rather than hiring a personal trainer (and would have probably had better results).

Social media is a fascinating modern form of documentation. It's a phenomenon that's reasonably new and its implications are still being worked into the fabric of our social lives. Being for or against social media is like being for or against air. Social media is multidimensional and has given us positives and negatives (which is a whole other book), but one use that is undeniably here to stay is using it to communicate.

Step 5. Storing and Leveraging: Organizing Your Personal Information

Our personal world is a great teacher of documentation practices because it cuts to life-or-death questions like "Where did we put the kids' passports?"

Apply the regular review process to your home office

The concept of a regular review cycle of your documentation is important for your personal life. Go back to key questions:

- What documents would you be stressed about losing? (e.g., birth certificates, tax slips, tax files)
- Which documents help your personal business? (e.g., key reference docs, marketing collateral, client files)
- Which documents are helpful in your life? (e.g., to-do lists, personal project files, idea files, writing projects)
- Which files could I move to archive? (e.g., old client files, manuals, house files)

I recommend you do an annual cleanup. Maybe it's during spring-cleaning or New Year's or at the end of your busy season.

The process shouldn't take more than a few hours and up to a day. Here are some suggestions:

- Step back and think about what is important to you.
- Remove papers and electronic documents you don't need.
- Think about and assess the personal documentation systems that are working or not working in your life (e.g., taxes, your calendar, family calendar, your to-do lists, ideas for your business, ideas for fun, administration files).
- Trash documents that are causing drag in your life.
- Attack things you haven't dealt with that you uncover in the process.
- Unearth and resurrect good ideas or projects you want to finish and put them in your calendar.

I recently did an annual cleanup of my documents. Most of my documents I didn't need. But I also found a few good ones that started to stir some thoughts and actions—an old financial plan that was still valid but hadn't been looked at, old ideas for articles I wanted to write, a course I wanted to take but never did (but still wanted to), old goals that made me laugh, and some great reference materials I had forgotten about. I also thought about a better system for organizing tax documents during the process.

I found skeletons in the closet along with the gems. The business ideas I launched that didn't work out. The clients that left. The proposals we never won. The drafts I needed to redo. The business cards (mine and people who have worked for me in the past) that were never used. Facing these "monsters" allowed me to let them go and freed me to tackle new challenges. That is the point of the process.

Step 6. Leading and Innovating: Making a Difference Outside the Office

Leading and innovating in our personal lives is about having more influence and impact on the things you care about outside of work, including your family, your friends, your hobbies, and your community. Leading and innovating when it comes to our personal lives is not about changing the world (unless you are Bill Gates) but about helping others you care about to be better.

It's a no-brainer that you can apply Dynamic Documentation to be a better leader for the people and the causes you care about. Your kids need structure and organization to get their homework and their piano practicing done. Your church needs help with the annual Christmas hamper drive. Your Paddleboard Association needs you to act as the treasurer. Your elderly parents need help organizing their paperwork. Use Dynamic Documentation practices to make yourself a better person and leader to the many people in your personal and home lives, too.

Innovation in your personal life is not about cutting-edge tools or techniques. It is about adding new habits and personality into your personal and home management practices and upping your game once in a while.

If you are a self-help junkie, perhaps you have lots of innovation already going on in your life. If you want to do some specific things that apply to documentation, here are just a few to help you:

- **Build your digital IQ:** Digital IQ means embracing new toys. You might be someone who does this naturally. Or you might need some push to make it happen. I personally need a push. Make yourself a digital IQ plan—find a new tip on LinkedIn, experiment with the tools in your calendar, call your help desk at work, or try out different Microsoft products for managing your finances or family schedule.

- **Experiment with apps and pen and paper for your to-do lists:** When it comes to your to-do list management, there are a ton of apps out there, many of which are free or inexpensive. Experiment with cool new apps and different options on your phone (including voice recording). But don't dismiss your pen and paper as archaic or ineffective. To-do apps may promise utopian management of your projects and daily tasks, but even tech-savvy reviewers have confessed to reverting to pen and paper after road testing various "best-in-class" apps. I personally use a combination of both old-school and new-school approaches and recommend you experiment with different systems that work for you.

- **Capture your ideas through a mix of tools:** Capturing your ideas is the fire-starter for life-changing events. In your personal world, you will probably need a mix of tools to capture ideas or things you should do that come into your head. The key here is that you are thinking of the ideas and are taking action to get them on paper. You can carry around a notebook, keep a journal by your bedside, use the notes section of your phone, or maintain a project list. There's an exciting new world of digital note-taking apps that you should check out, too. For blog or writing ideas, I have a "Blog and Ideas" file where I jot concepts and new insights so I don't lose any (rare but precious) strokes of genius that come my way. How many times have you had a brainstorm in the middle of the night, in the shower, or on the bus, and thought "Oh, I'll remember this; no need to write it down." And then, poof! That sparkle is gone, like a snowflake on an ice skater's nose.

As much as I love how Dynamic Documentation fuels my work, I'm equally or even more convinced of its essential role in my personal life. With a little effort, I see huge improvements in my ability to keep everything flowing and everyone happy (most of the time). I know that these small practices have an outsized impact on my life. I hope you'll test out the suggestions in this chapter in your own life and see how dynamic thinking, practices, and skills have far-reaching impact on your self-care, your home life, your family, and even your community.

CONCLUSION

Documentation is evolving. But, in some foundational ways, documentation practices haven't really changed from ancient times. Documentation has always been about preserving the past, controlling the present, and propelling the future. There will continue to be changes in technology, consumer trends, regulations, the workforce, and many other developments. But the principles will stay the same.

Following the 24-Hour Rule and other "secrets" and building your documentation skills will have a ripple effect on your personal life, work, and goals. Small (Little d) things such as capturing your ideas, having strong to-do practices, improving your focus, structuring your thoughts, following up with your clients and prospects, and strengthening your analytical skills will create a major impact on your career and your life.

Your organization will win big from your efforts, too. Your Big D projects such as large-scale systems, information governance projects, policies and procedures, and compliance and regulatory programs will benefit from the same Little d concepts, practices, skills, and tricks. You'll be solving the right problems with the right level of complexity, while making sure that your team's hard-earned work is actually *used*!

The practice of Dynamic Documentation will help you deliver more work and a higher level of quality and creativity. It will compel you to be a genuinely more helpful person at work, at home, and in your community. The concepts and language and mindsets of Dynamic Documentation will affect how you work with clients and colleagues as you develop the muscles to record notes, get on the same page with next steps and outcomes, and skill stack to make everything you do just a bit better, smarter, and faster.

Realistically, you are not going to implement everything in this book, at least not immediately. Not all guidance will be relevant to your current goals—though it could be someday.

It is my hope you enjoyed this book and found something useful to apply to your career, your life, and the organizations in which you work. I hope this has given you a new outlook on this vital but often underappreciated topic. I hope to continue this lasting conversation with you, too.

For more information and insights, please check out my website www .bellehumeurco.com, where you can sign up for my monthly newsletter. You can also follow me on LinkedIn, where I'll be sure to follow you back.

LinkedIn: @AdrienneBellehumeur
Website: www.bellehumeurco.com

Share what you've learned with others—and I'd love to hear about your big wins and challenges!

Good luck and happy documenting,

Adrienne

ACKNOWLEDGMENTS

The 24-Hour Rule took more than 5 years (and counting) to materialize. What started as a simple concept to help clients get a better handle on their documentation grew into a bigger and bigger project.

Firstly, thank you to my adoring (and adorable) husband, Neil. You took care of our three munchkins when I went to the office on Sundays to write this. You read my "nerdy" writing and gave feedback unconditionally. And you gave me my start (when we first met) to find meaningful consulting work and great clients. (And you are a good friend, too.)

Thank you to my dear friend and coach Jan Eden. You pushed me to write about documentation in the first place (twelve years ago, if you can believe it). You saw the vision for this book and the "new world of documentation" before I did. Thank you for your uncanny ideas. And thank you for forcing me to pick up the phone and call Janet Goldstein . . .

Thanks to Janet Goldstein—you are a book genius! You worked your magic through the difficult first drafts. You were patient and helpful at the same time and always able to unstick obstacles we bumped into. I have learned enormously from working with you and am forever grateful for all you have done for me.

Thank you to Marty Kleinman for your awesome and entertaining edits. You are a master storyteller. Thank you for bringing humor and fun to this topic.

To Taija Morgan, thank you for your wonderful editing at various stages of this book—including at the beginning, when it started as a pile of messy ideas.

on ，

To Alexandra Watkins, who came up with the name "Dynamic Documentation." It's perfect.

Thank you to Emily Sixta and Paul Nielsen at Faceout for your funky illustrations. You were wonderful to work with.

Thank you to Jayme Johnson and her team at Worthy Marketing for your support, creativity, and spunk. You helped make documentation appealing, lively, and amusing.

Thank you to the early readers of this book who provided feedback, including Ana Djuric, Miriam Clark, and especially Bob Sprague, who gave this book a pharmaceutical level of detailed review.

To Matt Holt at BenBella Books for taking on this project and to his team of awesome ladies—Katie Dickman, Brigid Pearson, Jessika Rieck, Mallory Hyde, Kerri Stebbins, Ariel Fagiola, and Leah Baxter.

Thank you to my amazing clients. If I didn't have you, I wouldn't have a business. You have taught me everything in this book by giving me a chance.

To my little kids, Claire, Bruce, and Gwen, and my big stepkids, Carson and Parker. I'm sure this book won't interest you today, but hopefully it will one day.

Thank you to my in-laws, Peggy and John, who are always helping out at our chaotic house.

To my parents for being the best. You gave me every advantage in school and sports. While you could never get me to clean my room, you should be happy to know that I've found peace and joy in organizing information and documents.

BIBLIOGRAPHY

Adams, Scott. *How to Fail at Almost Everything and Still Win Big: Kind of the Story of My Life.* New York: Penguin, 2013.

Adams, Sean. *Graphic Design Rules: 365 Essential Dos and Don'ts.* New York: Princeton Architectural Press, 2020.

Adams, Sean. "Introducing the Foundations of Layout and Composition." Graphic Design Foundations: Layout and Composition. LinkedIn Course, https://www.linkedin.com/learning/graphic-design-foundations-layout -and-composition/introducing-the-foundations-of-layout-and-composition ?autoplay=true.

Allen, David. *Getting Things Done: The Art of Stress-Free Productivity.* New York: Penguin, 2001.

Bezos, Jeff. *Invent and Wander: The Collected Writings of Jeff Bezos.* Boston: Harvard Business Review Press, 2021.

Brown, Karma. *The 4% Fix: How One Hour Can Change Your Life.* New York: HarperCollins, 2020.

Byrne, Rhona. *The Secret.* New York: Simon and Schuster, 2006.

Clark, Dorie. *The Long Game: How to Be a Long-Term Thinker in a Short-Term World.* Boston: Harvard Business Review Press, 2021.

Clear, James. *Atomic Habits: An Easy & Proven Way to Build Good Habits & Break Bad Ones.* New York: Avery, 2018.

Forte, Tiago. *Building a Second Brain: A Proven Method to Organize Your Digital Life and Unlock Your Creative Potential.* New York: Atria Books, 2022.

Grahl, Tim. *Your First 1000 Copies: The Step-by-Step Guide to Marketing Your Book.* Out:think, 2013.

Hallowell, Edward. "Overloaded Circuits: Why Smart People Underperform." *Harvard Business Review,* January 2005.

"How to Get Started with Enterprise Content Management." AIIM Course.

Jorgenson, Eric. *The Almanack of Naval Ravikant: A Guide to Wealth and Happiness.* Magrathea Publishing, 2020.

Kondō, Marie. *The Life-Changing Magic of Tidying Up: The Japanese Art of Decluttering and Organizing.* Berkeley: Ten Speed Press, 2014.

Maslen, Andy. *Write to Sell: The Ultimate Guide to Great Copywriting.* Marshall Cavendish Corporation, 2009.

Miller, George A. "The Magical Number Seven, Plus or Minus Two: Some Limits on Our Capacity for Processing Information." *Psychological Review* 63.2: 81–97.

Ries, Eric. *The Lean Startup.* New York: Crown Business, 2011.

Sibbet, David. *Visual Meetings: How Graphics, Sticky Notes and Idea Mapping Can Transform Group Productivity.* Hoboken: Wiley, 2010.

Zinsser, William. *On Writing Well: The Classic Guide to Writing Nonfiction.* 30th Anniversary Edition. New York: Harper Perennial, 2006.

INDEX

ABOUT THE AUTHOR

Adrienne Bellehumeur is the founder of Bellehumeur Co. and copartner of Risk Oversight, based in Calgary, Alberta, a leading firm in Internal Controls, Internal Audit, and Compliance. In her 15 years of experience as a consultant and business owner, she has developed, practiced, and taught Dynamic Documentation to tackle business analysis assignments, SOX programs, audits and review engagements, Information Management projects, system implementations, technical and proposal writing, communications, change management advising, and much more.

Driven to help companies—and individuals—enhance their productivity, Adrienne believes everyone can work smarter, faster, and better, and that momentum comes from clarity and action.

She has worked with myriad professionals—accountants, lawyers, engineers, administrators, sales professionals, project managers, IT people, and small business owners—and she has tackled hundreds of client projects and (of course) many documents.

As a working woman with three kids (ages eight and under), two older stepkids, a dog, a dragon (it's a lizard in the basement), and (let's not forget) a husband, she is passionate about working hard and playing hard and puts the secrets of the 24-Hour Rule into practice every day. She brings her expertise and smarts to a range of workshops, trainings, speaking opportunities, and consulting engagements with teams who want to solve problems using the right techniques.

WORK WITH US

BELLEHUMEUR CO.
Make your company smarter, faster, better.
Documentation Consulting and Services, Training, and Speaking

Dynamic Documentation is an investment that pays off. It's a measurable, leverageable business asset that leads to clarity, momentum, cost-savings, and, ultimately, growth. Bellehumeur Co. can help you mine your ideas and boost the knowledge of your organization with training and services including:

- Process documentation and mapping
- Process improvement and optimization
- Information management and governance
- Business analysis and problem-solving
- Technical writing, document creation, and review
- Documentation training and workshops
- Speaking opportunities

For more information, resources, and tools, visit: www.bellehumeurco.com.

RISK OVERSIGHT
A better response to risk.
Internal Audit and Controls, Governance, Risk, and Compliance Programs

Risk Oversight brings deep expertise in managing, overseeing, consulting, testing, and advisory specifically for audit and internal control programs. Our philosophy is based on common sense, lean, and fit-for-purpose internal control, audit, compliance, and risk management programs that deliver the highest possible value for our clients. We have extensive experience in running:

- SOX, CSOX, Internal Control over Financial Reporting (ICFR) programs
- Internal audits and outsourced internal audit functions
- Compliance and regulatory related initiatives
- Risk management programs
- IT audits and assessments

For more information, resources, and tools visit: www.riskoversight.ca